How To Write Words That Sell

Create Your Own Money Making Ads, Sales Letters, Email and Social Media Hacks

Jim McCraigh

A No-Nonsense Marketing Guide™

Copyright 2014 Jim McCraigh and Business Growth Strategies

All rights reserved. No part of this book may be reproduced in any form without permission in writing from the author. Reviewers may quote brief passages in reviews. Readers may share this document with fiends only if it the entire, unedited document is shared.

Disclaimer and FTC Notice

No part of this publication may be reproduced or transmitted in any form or by any means mechanical or electronic, including photocopying or recording or by any information storage and retrieval system or transmitted by email without permission in writing from the publisher.

While all attempts have been made to verify the information provided in this publication, neither the author nor the publisher assumes any responsibility for errors or omissions or contrary interpretations of the subject matter.

This book is for entertainment purposes only. The views expressed are those of the author alone, and should not be taken as expert instruction or commands. The reader is responsible for his or her own actions.

Adherence to all applicable laws and regulations including international federal, state and local governing professional licensing, business practices, advertising and all other aspects of doing business in the US, Canada or any other jurisdiction is the sole responsibility of the purchaser or reader of these materials.

Any perceived slight of any individual or organization is purely unintentional.

Every link to products are those that I've personally used and/or found useful. Please do your own research before making any purchase online. There are no affiliate links in this book.

Contact the Jim at jim@mccraigh.com

Find his blog at http://www.mccraigh.com

ISBN-13: 978-1502465252

ISBN-10: 1502465256

To my wife Shelley,

who has always been supportive,

enthusiastic and interested...

Need More Clients Now?

Grab this FREE eBook!

Accelerate the process of getting new clients with *7 Simple Ways to Get Clients Now.* Like the book you are reading now, it's full of trips and tricks that I've learned over nearly three decades of successfully marketing my services and those of others!

Download it FREE at http://eepurl.com/bbL3kH

Table of Contents

A Gift for You 5

1: Before You Write Anything 11

2: Crafting Profitable Headlines 15

3: Convincing Them Why They Should Care..47

4: Making and Proving Claims 57

5: Make an Offer They Can't Refuse 66

6: Ask Them to do Something Easy 76

7: Sales Letter Mojo..81

8: Building or Renting Lists 93

9: Crafting Profitable Print Ads 117

10: Creating Money Making Brochures 127

11: Power Editing Your Sales Copy 133

12: Writing Effective Web Copy 137

13: Social Media Hacks 150

14: Wildly Successful Email...........................158

BONUS Section 164

BONUS Book Excerpt 170

Until now, most books available on writing ads, sales letters, and brochures were based on concepts developed in the 1920's and 1930's. Those writers and prospects lived and worked in a time and place that was incredibly different than today's wired 21st century world. Many of the principles advanced in those books are timeless, as useful today as they were then, but the application of those truths has changed dramatically. This book shows you how to do just that!

- *Jim McCraigh*

An Easy and Profitable Formula

Successful ads, letters, emails, brochures and web pages all have a common structure and organization. Here's my five step method for writing your own money making copy. These apply to almost all types of advertising writing, sales letters, ads, brochures and web sites. Once you have mastered these 5 elements, money making copywriting will become second nature for you!

- Use a powerful headline to capture the reader's immediate attention

- Convince them why they should care

- Prove your claims

- Make them an offer they can't refuse

Ask them to do something that's safe and easy

Think of this list as a ready-made outline for all of your copywriting efforts.

1: Before You Write Anything

You are probably anxious to get started, but in copywriting as in house painting, preparation is the key to a good job. There are three fundamental questions you must ask yourself before you write any sales letter, FaceBook ad, email, web page or whatever you are working on.

So before you write a word, take the time to completely answer them. Doing so will help boost the response to what you write:

- What are you selling?

- What problem does it solve?

- Who are you selling it to?

Let's examine each one in detail...

What Are You Selling?

This may not be as simple as it sounds. Does Federal Express sell air courier service? Or do they offer the assurance that your package will arrive before 10:30 am the next day? Does Volvo sell automobiles or do they sell safety? Did Domino's become a successful company by selling pizza, or was it fast delivery? By now you've probably guessed that it is the latter in all three cases. These companies have prospered by selling the benefits of their product or service. What are you selling? If you can't answer this question in 8 words or less, you are not ready to write. If you need help with this, read the section on benefits first.

TIP: The best copywriters remember that they can never sell two things at once. Make sure that each ad, sales letter, or web site you write has only ONE compelling theme or idea you wish to communicate.

What Problem Does it Solve?

In order to generate the best results, your product or service must solve a problem that your target market perceives that they have... and are willing to spend money to solve. Let me explain it this way... what is it that keeps your prospect awake at night? If you don't know the answer to this question... find out. Knowing this one piece of information will pay you huge dividends.

Who are You Selling it to?

If "everyone" is a possible prospect for your product or service, then it is likely that almost no one will buy it. You must precisely define the exact profile of your target prospect. The mass marketing techniques of the 1950's, 60's and 70's have outlived their usefulness. General circulation periodicals like the Saturday Evening Post and Life Magazine were in almost every home, making it easy to reach "everyone". Direct mail campaigns were directed at broad-brush groups such as "young families", "homeowners", or "professional people". Daytime TV was targeted at women. That's as far as it went. There weren't many choices.

In the 1980's society became more diverse, advertisers began to find success by dividing or segmenting broader markets into audiences of separate communities. Appeals were developed to engage bicyclists, snow skiers, antique collectors, wine connoisseurs, auto enthusiasts, pet owners and hundreds of other specific groups. Special interest magazines, cable television programs and highly targeted mailing lists became the tools of sophisticated marketers in search of higher returns on money spent.

In the 1990's, advances in desktop computers ushered in database marketing. Customers and prospects habits could be tracked, analyzed and utilized to increase capture rates. Buying patterns could be tailored to specific offers sent to individual consumers. These days, the increasingly widespread use of the internet actually lets prospects identify themselves as a potential customer through a marketer's web site by sharing their email address and giving you permission to contact them. Once you have answered these three questions, you are ready to write!

2: Crafting Profitable Headlines

Read this section and you will discover the secrets of powerful and effective headlines. Ignore it and you may as well skip the rest of this book. Your headlines will account for 80% of your success or failure. Five times as many people read the headline as read the ad or letter. You get the point...

Changes in headlines have produced documented increases of 100%, 200% or even more in response rates. Great headlines are the key to breaking through the clutter of hundreds of thousands of advertising messages that we all see and hear during the course of a single year. If you are only going to read part of this book, make it this part!

These days, prospects and customers are bombarded with hundreds of advertising messages every day. Television, radio, magazines, newspapers, direct mail, phone calls, web sites, newsletters, emails, grocery carts, and bus benches provide people with more daily advertising impressions than they can possibly absorb. After half a lifetime or so at this level, many people simply ignore or tune out advertising as a defense mechanism. So how do you get their attention? ...By using effective, attention getting headlines.

Here's a secret that all successful copywriters know: You can go from losing money to making a ton of cash just by changing a few words. What words are those? The first words in any letter, ad or web page... The headline!

Recently, I had this proven to me beyond a shadow of a doubt. About a year ago, a new client called me to say that she had to cancel our phone consultation that day because part of her website was down and that she would reschedule as soon as the problem was resolved. After I hung up, I went to her site to find her shopping cart working perfectly. I called her back immediately to relay the good news. She told me it was still down as she had not received any sales for two days and something must be dreadfully wrong. I asked her if she had changed anything else. She said that she had improved the graphic look of the site. I went back to the sales page to discover that her headline had been replaced with a graphic. Once she replaced the old headline, the flow of subscriptions began once again. The simple act of removing the headline took her response rate to ZERO! Putting it back got things going again. Is this an extreme example? Maybe... but what increase in response could you achieve by the addition of an effective headline to your sales letters, ads, brochures, email or web pages?

We have been conditioned to decide what to read based on the effect a few choice words have on our thoughts and our feelings. With books, it's the title. With the newspaper, it's the headlines. With a magazine on the newsstand, it's the teasers on the cover. We decide to read ads, letters, email and web pages in the same way.

Knock your Socks Off Headlines

A great headline should have all the target seeking power of a smart bomb that locks in on its target and explodes on impact. The reality of our fast paced world is that you have just two seconds to get their attention. (Forget the old four second rule... it's too long, the world moves twice as fast now). If you don't, you'll lose the reader in a heartbeat. Make sure your headline is crystal clear and promises a real benefit so the reader will respond positively.

"How A Simple Change To Your Ad Copy Can Increase Your Sales By 100% Or More"

Did this get your attention? Of all the components of your copy that you can change to improve your results, the headline carries the most weight. The headline is the most crucial component of your copy. It bears the responsibility of pulling people into your ad, sales letter, or web marketing piece. If you can't attract people's attention and convince them to read further, you won't make many sales. And the rest of the ad or letter won't matter at all.

Test after test has proven that a promotional piece with a headline - any headline - will outperform a promotional piece without a headline. And if you can craft a headline centered on the major benefit you bring to your customers, the difference in response can be astounding.

More than once I've seen just the change of a headline pull three times as much as an ad with a weaker headline. The copy and graphics were exactly the same. The offer was exactly the same. And the ad, sales letter, or web marketing piece reached precisely the same audience. The only change was a different headline. Improvements of that magnitude are just too good to pass up!

Why Headlines Are So Vital To Your Success

The way to cut through all this clutter and get your prospects' attention is to craft a headline that is so compelling, so interesting and so moving that it stops customers in their tracks! How do you accomplish this elusive task? By promising the customer whatever it is they want the most. That promise can be presented through the following techniques:

-The major benefit your customer receives

- A special, limited time offer

- A powerful testimonial

Of all the promises listed above, there is one that stands head and shoulders above the rest. In fact, in the vast majority of ads and sales letters I write, I use it as the focus of the headline. I might include other promises in the headline as well, but I always focus the headline on this particular type of promise.

Can you guess what it is? Well, I won't keep you in the dark. The single most effective promise to use in your headline is:

The solution to the one problem that keeps them awake at night...

Nothing more or less. Your customer only cares about how your product can solve a crucial, nagging problem they have... or how you can help them achieve an important goal. So why waste time with anything else? It's simple and it works almost every time. I've used the major benefit promise time and time again to help my clients sell millions of dollars worth of their products and services.

There is no other promise format that's safer to use. After all, who doesn't want to have their most pressing needs and wants satisfied? Ask yourself what your customers really want the most. (Later in this chapter I'll show you exactly how to do this.) The question is then, how do you write headlines that will make people want to buy?

The Ultimate Headline

Imagine for moment that you are driving alone on a dark, unfamiliar and deserted road. Suddenly you notice that your fuel gauge reads "EMPTY". You have that sinking feeling in the pit of your stomach. The last gas station was miles ago, probably more distance than you have gas to make it back. It's cold and raining. Your cell phone is at home. You begin to scan the horizon for signs of a service station. You see nothing but darkness as you drive on until you spot a billboard sign that reads "Acme Gasoline Gives You Better Performance" Big deal... that doesn't solve my immediate problem! Another appears on the horizon, "Ace Gasoline Burns Cleaner" Not interested. What you are looking for is a sign that reads: GAS 100 Yards Ahead ... Open 24 hours... All Credit Cards Accepted! That is the type of headline that gets results. It promises exactly what you want, when you want it! For our purposes, headlines can be classified into two very separate and distinct categories:

- Those that work

-Those that don't

Think of it like a soccer game. Either you get the ball into the goal or you don't. But, the difference between a headline that works really well and one that doesn't can be very subtle. Let's look at some specifics...

How to Craft Money Making Headlines

One of the first big successes I had as an ad copywriter came in the early 1970's when I was the young marketing director of a Chicago area bank. The project assigned to me was the opening of the bank's newly remodeled drive-through facility. I wanted to use a premium, but was given a modest budget of only $1.00 per item. (Hardly anything... even then!) After surveying ad specialty catalogs, I found nothing that seemed to make sense at that budget. A few days before the ad was scheduled to run I put my head in my hands, stared at the wall, and wondered how I would tell my boss I hadn't come up with anything.

Then it came to me! Since I'd started as a teller a couple of years earlier, I remembered that some regular customers would ask jokingly if I had any free samples. Then it hit me and without hesitation I wrote:

"Bank Finally Offers Free Samples: We'll Give You $1 to Try Our New Drive-Thru Banking Center"

The rest of the copy consisted of times, dates and location of the new facility. I closed the ad with a call to action, added the bank's logo, sent the ad out to be proofed and placed it for publication on the following Sunday. Early the next Monday morning, I was in my office with a loan applicant when I noticed a police officer approaching my open door. He seemed agitated. He quickly made eye contact with me and told me he needed to talk to me. I quickly excused myself with the customer and asked the officer if I could help him. "I wonder if I might see your city permit for the event outside?" I told him that our remodeling project had been signed off on by building inspectors weeks ago. "No", he said, "I mean for the cars lined up out of your parking lot, on to the street and blocking traffic!" My boss was so elated that he didn't seem to mind paying the city for two off duty police officers to direct traffic that day.

Since then, I've realized that if I was ever going to have that type of success again, then I'd darned well better find out WHY that headline worked.

Great headlines get your attention and promise a benefit all within the space of a few words. They appeal to an intense desire to gain something, such as increased income, social status, security, and love or show you how to avoid undesirable things like pain, financial loss, unnecessary work, or embarrassment. (I usually favor headlines that take the "fear of loss" approach... most people are more motivated to avoid loss than they are to do something for gain.) The best headlines go a step farther and suggest that the solution is simple and easy to obtain.

Great headlines DEMAND the target prospect stop and read them. They appeal to a specific individual, not everyone. They shout "this is for YOU, Bob." Great headlines select out those people who will be interested in your offer and cause them to read the rest of your copy. Great headlines raise eyebrows! The very best moneymaking headlines are often taken from the requests and words of your customers own mouths... Like my "free money samples".

Because your headline can be 80% of your success or failure, spend at least that much or more of your copywriting time on crafting your headline. Develop at least 15 headlines for each letter, ad, or web page you write and then write 5 more. It is extremely unlikely that the first headline or two that you write will be the best one possible. Be ruthless in your critique of what you write. By the way, those other headlines can form the basis of subheads in your body copy, so it's not just an exercise.

A headline is meant to do two very important things. First, it needs to grab the reader's attention… RIGHT NOW! I can't state this too strongly. All the ads, brochures, catalogs, flyers, direct mail pieces and web sites people see everyday are just a big blur to them. Your headline must be prominent and effective enough to pull the reader into the copy and lead them into reading further. To do that, it must cater to a specific emotion or a relevant condition… one to which the reader can easily associate. To illustrate, here's a list of "triggers". I did not develop this list… you have probably seen them before:

These are in rough rank order with the strongest first…

Fear, Pain, Loss, Health, Love, Greed, Longer Life, Pride, Power, Ego, Ease, Anger.

Get Their Attention with These Words

Typically, less than one out of five people will get beyond the headline to read the body of an ad… So spend the time to make your headline work. State a benefit in your headline that clearly enhances their life, using power words like:

Announcing, Breakthrough, Discover, Facts, New, Now, Sale, Yes, You, Free, Fast, Easy, Proven, Guaranteed, How to, Save, Increase, Secret, More, 54% (or any specific percentage of increase or decrease)

Sound familiar? That's because these words have been used before. Why? Because they WORK! Why question success? These words all are active, grab the attention of prospects, and promise them something. (The two words of most value to your customers are You and Free.) Some inexperienced copywriters avoid these words because they sound "old" or seem tired. They want to be more creative. Creativity can be a wonderful thing, but successful copywriting is about what works!

Writing Client-Centered Headlines

Prospects are in a hurry. They are bombarded with tons of ads, emails, postcards and commercials every day. They tend to skip or tune out any marketing message that looks as if it will take too much time or trouble to understand. So don't make your prospect read the whole ad to get the mail idea. You will lose them. Cut out unnecessary words. Put subheadings in your copy to break up stretches of text. Once the headline communicates that you have something readers are interested in, they will take more time to look at your letter, ad or web page. Company-centric headlines (ones about you) almost never work. Avoid them. They are the sign of a rank amateur.

Write to your prospects like they were the only ones reading it. Since your headline will be read by individual people, try to imagine one single person reading your message and being interested in your product or service. In fact, it will be much to your advantage to make your target customer as "real" as possible. There are some companies that go so far as to name their ideal customer and put a face to that name! I've heard of one company that actually used a mannequin in their marketing department that had the same characteristics as their target consumer. You probably won't go that far, but hey, what's wrong with a small photo clipped from a magazine and taped to your monitor? Continue writing your headline and ad with this one person in mind.

Write as if you are talking to them alone! The fact is that customers are far more interested in reading about THEMSELVES than about your company. It is all about your customer. Your headline gets attention when it appeals to the reader's interests. Use your headline to point out a problem the reader has or something you know the reader feels strongly about. Headlines are NOT the place to list the features of your product or service. Instead, get right to the point.

Here's a way to instantly sniff out ineffective copy before it ever goes to press. Read the headline (or first paragraph) of any ad, brochure or web page. If it is about the advertiser, it won't produce the results it should. The truth is that nobody cares about your company! I always cringe when I see this junk, because I know they are wasting their money.

While we are on this subject, here is another grabber headline I wrote while at the bank:

"100 Gallons of FREE Gasoline with Your Next Car Loan"

The free gas was the payoff to the customer for getting their loan from us. The ad worked magnificently... we made more car loans that month that anyone could remember. The bad news was that at that point in my career, I still did not know why my ads where working (or not working). It was hit or miss. It was only later that I learned the techniques that I am going to share with you in this book. (By the way... studies show headlines get even better results if they're enclosed in quotation marks like the 100 Gallon example above.)

Here is the compelling technique I mentioned that will change the way that you write benefit statements in headlines. Use it and you will increase your sales. The best news is it is not expensive to implement, in fact often you can do this for almost nothing. Do this:

ASK your customers (AND PROSPECTS) exactly why they BUY (or DON'T!) your product or service!

Ask them to tell you how they benefit. The answers may surprise you. Encourage them add other benefits that you may not have thought about. Let them tell you what the most important benefits are. How do you find this out? Take key customers to lunch. Call them, talk to them! You may be amazed at what they tell you! Remember, it's not what you think your product does, it's what the customer thinks!

A few years ago, while I was writing direct mail pieces for a seminar company, I would go to the seminars and talk to the attendees. I would ask them what about the mailer that prompted them to come. I also used an evaluation form that asked them to share the most valuable piece of information they learned from the program. I used their responses to craft the next mailers.

Then write a number of headlines based on what they have told you. Make up a list of the best six or seven and ask your customers and prospects to rank the headlines in the order for best to worst in terms of how well the headline appeals to them and motivates them to take action. You could do this in person or by mail, but you'll get faster results if you use an online tool like SurveyMonkey.com (I have no relationship with Survey Monkey other than as a user.)

What I am saying here is don't write your headlines (or any other copy) in a closed up room by yourself with a blank piece of paper! LET YOUR CUSTOMERS AND PROSPECTS HELP YOU!

Tip: There is an important difference between "needs" and "wants." Headlines that deal with needs will not perform as well as those that appeal to wants. We NEED a car, but we WANT to have our ego boosted with a flashy red sports model. What your prospect needs is not always the same as what they want.

Brainstorming Effective Headlines

Have writer's block? Use these simple and easy steps each and every time you want and need to create an effective headline. This brainstorming technique will help get your ideas flowing.

1.) Decide who you are writing to. The more specific you are, the more you can "speak" to them. Are they dentists, CEO's, building owners, barbers, police chiefs or network administrators? Be as specific as you can. Are they dentists who own their own buildings? If there are two groups, write two different headlines and marketing pieces. You can't be all things to all people. The more specific you are the more successful you'll be.

2.) Decide what benefits will be most important to prospective buyers of your product or service. How do you do this? Again, ask the people who have already purchased from you what they think. It's a very powerful tool you can use... but here is one that works even better... Ask those who have seen your offer why they did not buy! You won't have any trouble with this as people will enjoy giving you their opinions. Use this intelligence in crafting your headline.

3.) Since your ad, sales letter, brochure or web page will be read by individual people, try to imagine just one person reading your message. Continue writing your headline with this one person in mind. Write as if you are speaking directly to them alone.

4.) On a blank page, begin to write phrases with one benefit, and one or two power words from this list ... Fast, Free, Easy, Proven, Guaranteed, Discover, How to, Save, Increase, You, Your, Secret, More, 70% (any percent), $99.95 (or any dollar amount). For example:

- Discover How Dentists Can Save 50% on Rent

- Proven Ways Police Can Save 24% on Uniforms

- Free Book Shows How to Increase Barber's Pay 40%

5.) Brainstorm at least 15 headlines like this. Then convert your most powerful ones into one of the formats in the next section.

Proven Headline Formats

Once you have mastered packing benefits into your headlines, choose one of these proven formats for your creation:

Format Idea #1: Use Questions

"Suffering from Heartburn?" "Are Skyrocketing Employee Health Insurance Costs Keeping You Awake at Night?" Question headlines like these get the reader to answer it in their minds, automatically getting the prospect involved in your message. For example, heartburn sufferers will read further into your letter, ad or web site copy just to find out what answer or solution you provide. (Those without heartburn will not be drawn to your offer... but who cares... they are not buyers!)

Starting a letter with a question is a classic way to get your reader involved. A few years ago, I wrote a seminar mail piece aimed at accountants whose clients used QuickBooks® accounting software. I posed the question "Can You Correctly Answer these 7 QuickBooks® Questions?" That mailer worked because each question required a sentence or two to answer, and was directly related to the accountant's business. The seminar series was very well attended. Many of the attendees I talked to at the programs said that almost all of them had read all 7 questions. Most said they could not answer more than 1 or 2 of them and that's why they were at the seminar!

Format Idea #2:

Use a "How to so that you can _____" format

For example... "How to Buy a New Car without Getting Ripped Off." How-to headlines can work like magic. They are great for telling your story with a minimum of words. This is one of my favorite headline formulas. It can also be called a "bridge headline", one which is based on presenting a problem, making the problem urgent and pressing and then presenting a solution in the offer. It works because you promise to bridge the gap between a prospect's problem and its solution. A headline that shows a big gap exists creates greater urgency to buy. After reading a well crafted bridge headline, readers will want to know how they can close that gap. And the wider that gap is perceived to be, the greater the desire to close it will be. Why? Because wide gaps appeal to stronger emotions and motives than small gaps do.

The headline that instantly communicates a problem (i.e., a painful situation or a potentially painful one that may arise without the benefits of your offering) will have more impact than a similar headline that does not.

Format Idea #3: Use a Testimonial as a Headline

I've used these with great success. The recommendation of a satisfied customer will help convince others to buy from you. Your message will almost always be more powerful if it comes from someone besides yourself...

"I wish I would have come to this seminar years earlier... It would have saved me hours of tedious data entry!

... Sally Dimes, Central Heating and Air, Carbon City"

Always include the customer's full name and the city she lives in. Many readers won't believe a testimonial if they don't see a full name and location. Make sure you get permission to publish these letters as testimonials, along with the writers' names and addresses. Without a genuine name and address, a testimonial could be phony and everyone knows it. (Even worse, in certain circumstances it can be construed as mail fraud by postal authorities.) Start actively collecting specific testimonials from top customers, using their own words. Consider using their photo plus full name and address.

Format Idea #4: Use Headlines with Deadlines

Many people tend to put off taking action. If you don't get the prospect to act now, you may never get the sale. Headlines like "Save $1000 this Week Only" and "Get 25% off if You Buy Before June 3rd" help boost response rates.

Format Idea #5: Offer Something Free

Offering something like a "FREE 5 Part Cold Calling Mini-Course" is a powerful way to get lots of interested prospects. There is a myth that affluent or professional customers are turned off by free offers. Not true! Simply tailor your free offer to match the style of your customers or industry. You might subtly headline a "no-cost initial consultation". What this really does is give them a way to check you out before they commit to buying something.

Some Types of Headlines to Avoid

Not all headlines are created equal. Some just start out bad and can't be fixed. Here are four examples:

Curiosity Headlines

These headlines attempt to lure prospects into reading the ad by appealing to the reader's sense of curiosity. The truth is that almost all of these headlines fail miserably. Most readers simply won't take the time to find out what you are talking about. (Remember the 2 second rule!) They often just assume the payoff to them won't be worth the time they spend reading your ad. An example of a really horrible curiosity type headline might be… "Do You Know Why Our Customers Love Us?"

Here are other examples:

"Who Makes the Best the Best Bread in the Midwest?"

"How Many Breweries are there in Tampa?"

"Who is the Best Pest Control Company in Portland?"

You get the point. A lot of curiosity headlines are used every day, but few work as well as intended. Given the high cost of failure, why take the risk?

Negative Headlines

I recently saw the headline "Why Most Business Ventures Fail". Such gloom and doom can hardly be attractive or interesting to readers. Certainly better results might be obtained by concentrating on a more positive appeal like "Seven Simple Ways to Help Guarantee Your New Business is a Success!"

Cute or Funny Headlines

Here in the United States, we live in an increasingly diverse society, comprised of people from many different cultures, religions, and ethnic groups. At the same time, the internet is accessible to people in almost every other country on earth. For many people now, English is a second language. A lot of humor is based upon a common understanding and subtle use of language and learned popular culture. There is a huge risk that many people just won't "get it". Even worse, they could be insulted. Misunderstood advertising messages can actually cause negative feelings toward your company. Don't make it any harder to communicate with your readers than it already is! Even if you are a world class humorist skip the funny stuff and focus on what the reader wants instead.

Making Good Headlines Even Better

Consider an ad tested with these two headlines:

A) *"How to Avoid These Mistakes in Painting Your House"*

B) *"How to Paint Your House to Last 10 Years or More"*

The second out-performed the first by 16 percent.

Here is another example... same body copy, different headlines:

A) *"Warning to Dog Owners!"*

B) *"Keep Your Dog Safe This Summer"*

The second ad out-pulled the first by 61 percent.

Here's one more... one ad, tested with different headlines:

"Don't Swelter This Summer"

"Now You Can Afford Air Conditioning"

Which one do you think pulled best?

The point here is that one small change to a headline can cause it outperform another by a huge margin. Here is an example from an actual headline that ran for decades. Can you tell which one it is?

1. Do You Make These Mistakes in English?

2. Do You Make Mistakes in English?

There is only *one* word difference between these two headlines. Copywriting experts at the time were divided 50-50 on which one would produce the best results. The first one has the reader wondering if they make those mistakes, a possible source of embarrassment. Or they may read it to prove to themselves that they are actually in command of the English language and feel better about themselves. The second asks a question that can be answered with a simple yes or no, and does not engage the reader beyond that. As you correctly guessed by now, headline #2 was a flop. Headline #1 went on to become a huge moneymaker over many years for the company.

The key to improving your headlines is to TEST, TEST and TEST! Split testing is the most common way to test headlines or any ad... Sure, you can show them to employees and friends around the office for some directional feedback, but you'll never be sure which headline will actually outperform another without a true market test. For example, a direct mailer can be tested by printing half with one headline and the other half with another. Use a code on your materials to track results. If mailing, keep quantities mailed small at first until you are able to clearly identify which one works best. That way the bulk of the mailing can enjoy use of the best headline. (This is usually 5000 or fewer pieces or emails.) Change only the headline when you test, nothing else... not even the weight of the paper, day of the week, or ink color... or you won't be able to best tell what caused any difference in response.

When you think that you have a really good headline, run with it for a while. Then test it against others at some point see if you can find another that outperforms it. Top marketers will continually test even top performing headlines to see if they can improve upon their success! If you are really serious about testing your headlines, create a fresh point of view by using a second copywriter to develop alternative headlines! Never be satisfied until you have a world class winner on your hands!

A Fast and Easy Way to Write Compelling Headlines

Sometimes you don't have all week, or even all day to craft money making headlines. Here's a secret used by many professional copywriters that you can use. Start and maintain a file of successful ads or sales letters. (How do you know they're successful? If you see them running for months or even years in the exactly the same format... they are successful!) Almost all copywriters do this. They recycle and they adapt. (Of course, complete ads must never be copied literally. There's a big difference between plagiarism and modeling.) But ideas can be easily adapted to fit your market, your offer and your message.

Where do you find the best ads to turn them into templates or "fill-in-the-blanks" formulas? Buy a couple tabloids, like The Star or The National

Enquirer or some of the more popular women's magazines. Look at the teasers on the cover as well as the ads... The tone and tenor of many of the ads may not fit with your market, but you will be changing them to match your situation anyway. Here is the lesson... Ad space in these publications is VERY expensive. If an ad is repeated in more than three to four issues, the ad is likely profitable. Rip out the ad and put it into your "keepers" file. Then convert your collection into "fill-in-the-blanks" formulas. Hey... why re-invent the wheel?

However, obvious clones of popular ad campaigns can work against you. Consider all the variations of the Diary Industry's well-known and long running "got milk?" campaign. I am so sick of seeing people copy it. Chances are high that that theme is not the best for your particular business. In fact, it probably isn't. Why go with something so overdone when you can be unique?

"Fill in the Blanks" Headlines

Why start with a blank page. You'll be more productive if you use templates. Here's a list of "thought provokers" to get you started. Remember to link each back to a benefit:

How to _____ So that You Can _____

The Best Kept Secret in _____ Lets You _____

Quiz: Test Your _____ Smarts

Discover the 7 Things That Guarantee _____

Good News for _____

How to Bounce Back from _____

How to Get Other People to _____

How to Handle _____

How to Make _____ Work for You

How to Turn _____ into _____

Mastering the Art of _____

No More _____

Questions and Answers About _____

They Didn't Think I Could _____ , But I Did!

Straight Talk About _____

The Amazing Solution for _____

What's HOT and NOT in _____

_____ and Grow Rich

_____ on the Cheap

Ways to Get More from Your _____

No-Fail Strategies for _____

Secrets to Successful _____

Ways to Jump-Start Your _____

Questions You Must Ask When _____

Time-Tested Tips for _____

Ask yourself... Does my headline effectively stop people, capture their attention and trigger their EMOTIONS in order to pull them into the copy? If not re-write it until it does. But save the ones you don't use as headlines, they could be great subheads... more on that elsewhere in this book.

Make Your Headline Pass this Brutal Test

Here's a test that professional copywriters use. Imagine all you were allowed to do was run your headline along with a phone number... as a little 2 x 3 inch advertisement. Would it work? Try it! If it does, you have a potential winner on your hands.

Headlines... Not Just for Ads Anymore

Every one of your marketing tools needs a headline. Sales letters, brochures, ads, web pages alike... all of them need one. It drives me nuts when I see an ad or brochure that features the company's logo as the lead item. What a waste of time and money! Nobody really cares about your logo. Work hard to craft provocative, attention grabbing headlines for all your writings. Make your headlines work hard to communicate your main benefits quickly and lead your prospect into the copy below. The stronger these headlines, the more powerful the pull. It will be worth it!

3: Convincing Them Why They Should Care

As I mentioned in the previous section on headlines, your prospects are constantly deluged with advertising messages. They just don't have time to read them all. Add that to the fact that they are jaded after seeing years of false advertising claims. These days, you literally have to fight for their attention.

What your prospects really want to know is who cares, why bother and what's the point? That's why you've got to write every ad, letter, and web page with the assumption that -- within 2 seconds -- the prospect will decide to read on or ignore your message entirely... UNLESS IT PROMISES A BIG, BOLD, BRASH BENEFIT! However, once you have captured their attention, you have to keep it!

What this means is that your OPENING is just about as important as your headline. Here's why... Once you get your prospects past your first two or three paragraphs... once you get them over that critical hill, there's a MUCH greater chance that they'll read your entire message.

That's why you should spend hours writing just the opening of an ad, letter, or web page. That's because it's not enough just to describe what you're selling. You need words, phrases, and questions that force your prospects to keep reading. You've got to make them so afraid of "missing out" so that they literally can't ignore your offer! So, once you've captured your prospects' attention with a compelling headline, your task is to draw them in FURTHER with an opening that holds a death grip on them.

By opening, I mean the first paragraph or two of your sales letter, ad, brochure or web site. When your opening is truly compelling, your prospects never get the chance to "decide" if they should keep reading. They just do it, without ever making a conscious decision.

Another way to think of the opening is as an "executive summary" of sorts... a condensed version of the entire message in the first one or two paragraphs. Hold nothing back... go all out... You don't get a second chance to hold their attention.

Here's an illustration from a letter I recently received in the mail. (You do read all direct mail, ads and brochures you receive, don't you? You should be opening each and analyzing it!)

Can You Imagine Being Hungry Enough to Eat Sawdust?

"Right now, thousands of families in southern Africa have so little food that they are reduced to eating sawdust, grass and boiled leaves. Southern Africa is in the midst of its worst food shortage in over 60 years. More than 14 million people face starvation in the coming months. Women and children, especially HIV/AIDS orphans, are among the most vulnerable. You'd be surprised by how far your contribution could go: $100 could provide grain to feed 6 families for 6 months!"

Here the writer's opening continues the strength of the compelling headline while transitioning into the body of the letter. Notice that after reading just the first few lines that you knew exactly what the writer wanted you to do. However, what's missing is a more overt statement of the benefit to the reader of making such a contribution. Still, it does pack a powerful emotional punch.

The main point here is that you be direct. I've seen copy with funny stories, information about the owners, or other distracting statements that don't demonstrate to the reader the major benefit of what they are selling.

By the way, when you increase your sales and income using what you have learned in this book; consider giving some of it to someone less fortunate. It will make me proud!

Here's another better example:

How to Sell a Whole Lot More of Your Consulting Services... And Eliminate One of Your Biggest Headaches at the Same Time!

Now there is a simple software program (created by a CPA) that can jump start your business into high gear – and make your life a whole lot easier at the same time!

Can your practice use thousands of dollars of additional sales? Would you like to achieve this while plugging one your biggest profit leaks at the same time?

If so, I know you'll find this material to be enormously valuable. Because I'm going to show you precisely how to pull in tons of new client work and dump one of your biggest time wasters... both at the same time!

Tip: See how there is no time wasted getting right to the point and immediately zeroing in on what's in it for the reader? (Remember our two second rule!) No fluff, no filler, just a clear restatement of the primary benefits.

Stressing Benefits

Most sales copy I review these days stresses features and advantages over benefits. Here's what's involved in developing compelling benefits...

First is an understanding of the difference between features, advantages and benefits:

Features ... "What products and services have"

For example, "This accounting software has a payroll module"

Advantages ... "What those features do"

For example, "This accounting software will allow you to do your payroll in your own office"

Benefits ... "What the advantages mean"

For example, "You will save time and money over using a payroll service"

As I mentioned in the headline section, benefits must appeal to an intense desire to gain something, such as increased income, social status, security, and love or show you how to avoid undesirable things like pain, financial loss, unnecessary work, or embarrassment. Contrary to popular thinking, clearly communicated true benefits are not vehicles for creating hype or puffery. They are an effective means through which customers can fully understand and appreciate a product's true purpose. Without compelling benefits, they just won't care and that means your expensive materials are headed right for the trash bin.

Openers and Transitional Phrases

One of the more challenging aspects of writing sales copy is making a smooth transition from one thought to a totally different one. It helps the reader to make the connection of... "What the heck does this have to do with that?"

Here's a list of openers as well as some transitional phrases to link subsequent paragraphs to the main ideas. Keep these handy for your next copywriting project.

Think about _____

____ often is the difference between success and failure

In today's economy _____

For well under $100, you can _____

Can you use _____

Here's a secret most business people don't know ____

Are you still _____ ?

How secure is your _____

Who can put a price on _____ ?

No you can _____

Let's face it _____

Wouldn't you like to _____ ?

Have you ever laid awake at night worrying about _ ?

Tired of the same old _____

You've probably noticed that _____

Classic Transitions:

- I'm sure you'll agree that

- In addition,

- And, that's not all

- But, that's just the beginning

- Think about it

- Here's why

- You might be asking yourself

- Here's what I mean

- How will this affect you?

- You'll also receive

Write Copy from the Reader's Point-of-View

Time is precious. Very few people will spend much time on your message if they do not see immediately that it has a direct benefit to them. If you make the mistake of writing about your own self-interest (what would benefit you or your company, rather than what will benefit your visitor), you'll only guarantee that your copy will be ineffective at best and a disaster at worst.

To keep your prospects at a peak level of interest, your copy must be written from their point of view. Specifically, you must always prove to the reader what's in it for them. What do they gain (or not lose) by purchasing your product or service? What critical problems can you solve for them? How can you make their life easier? How can you make their life better? How can they make more money? How can their income go farther or reduce their expenses?

These are the underlying wants and needs that all people long to have fulfilled. It's all about an EMOTIONAL connection, not a logical one. These are the real reasons why most people will answer your ad, respond to your sales letter, or buy from your web site!

4: Making and Proving Claims

Your promise is everything. What do I mean by everything? It is nothing short of being the key to your ongoing long term success. There are two components to a powerful claim we'll cover here:

Making a Remarkable Promise (THE CLAIM)

If you want to be a success in the business of writing your own sales copy, you must learn break through the fog of reader complacency. How? By you making a remarkable promise. You have to promise something absolutely huge - something that stretches your reader's most realistic expectations. Ho-hum claims just don't cut it anymore in our cynical world. To bring anything to market with the following pitch... "Hey... This is a pretty good product. At least as good as anything out there. Why don't you try it?"... That is marketing suicide.

... And Then Make it Completely Believable (THE PROOF)

At the same time, you can't stretch expectations beyond the boundary of what's believable. Your goal is to lead your prospect right up to the boundary of believability... then stop just short of that boundary and prove your claim. To accomplish this, offer a convincing argument that forces the reader to believe the promise you've just made.

Let's take a closer look at an actual claim and see how you can accomplish this:

"Serious about making staggering profits on your precious metals investments? Above average returns can be hard to come by... New Report Details Seven Proven Techniques that can Produce Astounding Levels of Profit Increase of up to 200 - 300%! We Guarantee it or Refund your Purchase Price..."

In this example, the promise begins with the tag line above the headline. "If you are serious about making staggering profits on your precious metals investments..." Doesn't leave much to the imagination does it? But at the same time, it plants a seed of doubt. Anyone who is interested will probably want to find out more before plunking down their hard-earned cash for this offer. What does "staggering" mean anyway? Where does this promise come from?

Is it too good to be true? Can I really count on that sort of results? What's the catch?

The most effective promise you can offer is an assurance of the major benefit your customer wants. Why fool around with anything else? Remember, you have only two seconds to break through the clutter and seize your reader's attention. The most forceful clutter buster you can use is to identify and shout out that one thing your reader covets the most. In this case it is increased profits from metals trading.

With the promise clearly telegraphed, the next line is a reality check. It starts by stating an undisputed fact that anyone with any experience in precious metals knows is true, "Above average returns can be hard to come by..." The purpose of this statement is to add credibility and believability to the copy. It is about taking the reader to the edge of believability and them bringing them back a bit. It get them closer to agreement that what you are promising is reasonable.

Next comes a statement of the main promise.

For example:

"New Report Details Seven Proven Techniques that can Produce Astounding Levels of Profit Increase of up to 200 - 300%."

You get the idea... Now let's make it totally believable.

Achieving Complete Believability

Are your claims believable? Some claims, although 100% true may not be believable. At this point, the reader's acceptance of the promised returns has probably been stretched nearly to the breaking point. So it must be followed with an equally powerful proof that this can actually be accomplished.

Are your claims reasonable? Will people buy your claims, or will they see them as a bunch of hype? (Hype is generally defined as "claims made without credible proof.)

Believability is enhanced when:

The reader is promised an increase in their current returns of up to 200 to 300% or their entire purchase price will be refunded. Notice that we are not promising 200 - 300% returns on their precious metal investments, but a 200 to 300% increase in their current level of profit. That is a reasonable expectation, while achieving profits 200 to 300% is probably not.

The specific number of "7 techniques" is used here to assure the reader that it's not just one or two ideas, but a number of methods that indicate depth of material. Specifics will outsell generalities. If you were writing this headline, do consider listing the seven topics in your body copy without giving them away.

The word "proven" adds strength here. Back it up with the use of specific and compelling testimonials. (See the next section for how to do this.)

You add a strong guarantee to the mix. (I cover guarantees later in this chapter.)

Use Compelling Testimonials for More Credibility

People like to do business with those that they know, like and trust... unfortunately building such credibility can take time. You can accelerate the process with the help of others through their testimonials. Take advantage of human nature by getting and using testimonials from satisfied customers.

The best testimonials are specific and results oriented. Quotes like "Excellent, Great Service or Really Interesting" mean little as they are vague and don't relate to benefits. Customers don't usually do a very good job of writing testimonials, so you have to help them. When a customer compliments you, ask if you can write it up for their signature. Most people will agree.

Here's an example:

"Your online Mustang parts source has saved me countless hours searching catalogs and parts houses. I found the '69 engine mounts I needed for my last project in just 7 minutes!"

-Steven Smith, Quality Auto Crafters, Farmer City, IL

This is a winner... Testimonials mean more when the specific name and location of the writer is included and are more likely to be viewed as genuine. Plus it is specific... the reader can see how the writer benefited and can easily see from the descriptive text how they too could have a similar experience. (As with all testimonials, always maintain copies of their signed letters in your office files.)

You can further strengthen testimonials by using pictures of your satisfied customers alongside their testimonials. When you do receive a good testimonial from a customer, always ask for a picture. This helps by associating a "real person" with the words, and makes it clear that these are real testimonials.

Guarantees Help Build Credibility and Sales

Do you offer an ironclad guarantee? If you don't, you'll lose profits. People need to feel assured they can get their money back if something goes wrong, especially when they're buying through the mail or internet.

Don't be afraid to restate your guarantee in more than one way in the same place. For example in the same sentence you might say something like: "Full Money Back Guarantee... Unless you are absolutely thrilled with our weed control service, we'll give you a complete refund of 100% of the entire purchase price." The terms of the guarantee were repeated twice... clearly communicating they will not have a problem!

Resist watering down your guarantee... continue to make it stronger as time goes on. Study the guarantees of your competitors and craft a better one. (I've even used guarantees in excess of the purchase price... and premiums they can keep even if they exercise their right to return the merchandise.) Then trumpet the fact that you have the foremost guarantee in the business. If you can't live up to a super strong guarantee, maybe you should rethink your product or service!

More on Guarantees

One component of a really powerful offer is to make your offer as risk-free as possible. Nobody wants to make a mistake and be stuck with something that doesn't deliver as promised. That's why you should make every effort to lift the risk from the prospect and place it squarely on your shoulders.

Make a bold guarantee and make it for as long as possible. If you have a quality product, you shouldn't worry because return rates will almost always drop the longer you extend your guarantee. How long or how bold should your guarantee be? As long as the incremental profit from the increased sales you get using a more liberal guarantee is greater than the expense of any returns, it's worth it!

Another effective guarantee strategy is offering a 30-day "hold-your-check or charge slip" trial. That means people will send you checks postdated 30 days out or you won't charge their credit cards for 30 days. This is particularly effective in mail order or internet selling.

Marketing-by-the-Facts

When novice copywriters don't bother to dig for facts, they fall back on vague generalizations and puffed-up claims to fill the empty space on the page. The words sound nice, but they don't sell much because the copy doesn't inform or motivate. Facts always sell more than hype.

As you do a final review of your completed copy, ask yourself... Did I substantiate all the claims I made? Did I back up my statements with proof in the form of statistics, graphs, pictures and testimonials? Am I providing my prospect with the information they need to make an informed decision? Or... am I just blowing smoke?

5: Make an Offer They Can't Refuse

In this section, I'm going to show you the secrets of crafting one of the most crucial components of your marketing piece... a compelling offer, the fourth of the five critical elements of a successful marketing message.

The late Steve Jobs, former CEO of Apple Computers once said "It's not enough to make your offer great, it has to be INSANELY great". Incremental improvements over your competition's offers, or even your own previous offers, don't cut it. Think about at making it at least twice as good! So what do you do if your offer is not markedly superior to everything else in your marketplace? Change it! Take whatever time you need to figure out how to make what you sell the "best in show" before you spend another penny on printing and postage.

It's Not the Product... it's the Offer!

There are basically three types of offers you can use. The first two will get you mediocre results. The third can become a virtual gold mine for your business!

(I'm only listing the first two to explain why they don't work.)

Passive offers are those that don't seem to promise much of anything. "Buy Now During Our Big Easter Blow Out!"; Announcing the Opening of our Main Street Bank!"; or "Join us Today!" There may be an offer there, but it's really hard to find. They don't motivate the reader to DO anything. There's no strong call to action with limp offers like these.

Negative offers threaten loss from inaction. "Renew Now and Keep Your Subscription Current"; "Don't Lose Out on This Offer That Can't Be Repeated!"; or "Don't Risk Financial Disaster... Get This Health Insurance Today!" I'll grant you that people will do more to avoid loss than to gain something... but these types of statements are clinchers that only help motivate an already interested reader to take action. They're not generally enough by themselves to cause cold prospects to reach into their pocket or purse and pull out their hard-earned cash.

When properly constructed, positive, action oriented offers will definitely boost response rates. Positive offers build on the attractive promise of your headline. They tell the reader in no uncertain terms how they will clearly benefit by responding to your message.

Positive offers take your proposition out of the realm of being a "sales pitch" and instead make it more like a profitable agreement between two friendly parties. Positive offers make it easy for the reader to say yes, and almost impossible to say no!

Positive offers give rather than take. Consider this typical tired, worn out offer for a vacation package that includes the usual hotel, air fare, activities, and ground transportation at a stale sounding "Special 25 percent discount!" Readers think... 25% off of what anyway? They have no point of reference from which to determine if this is a good deal or not. Into the trash it goes!

Instead, the offer can be recast as a positive one to significantly increase response: "Book by March 31st and we'll pay for your hotel room... a $670 value!" Now the reader understands exactly what's in it for them. Now you have their attention... but it's still not enough. You can get even more response by adding what I call "Add-Ons and Take-Aways."

Add-Ons work by heaping on bonus after bonus until finally the reader has to say OK! Enough! Stop!" and take out their charge card. The old Ginsu Knife® commercials used this technique perfectly to sell millions of dollars of cutlery. The announcer would say "And if you act now you'll also get..." and then about 10 more different knives and kitchen gadgets would pop up on the screen. It made you think about how much you got for such a little price. That's the power of the "Add-On". Think BIG value and LITTLE price.

With this travel package example, you could add a free wine and cheese party AND a free T-shirt, AND free sailing class, AND a free beach towel. Then you could make deals with other businesses where they'd let you give away one of their products or services to your customers as a trial device to bring your customers to them. If you really use your imagination here you'll come up with lots of ways to create your own "Add-Ons". You get the picture... it's an offer your prospects can't refuse... and it gets your phone ringing!

"Take Aways" are price reductions after you have presented your price to the reader. They work like this... you bring they reader to the call to action... the decision point. You quote the price of $99.00. Then in the next line of copy, reduce it to $79.00 if they order by a specific deadline. This has two effects; first, it motivates those who may not be quite sure they want to buy at $99, and provides an "urgency kicker" (and even more value perception) for those that were willing to buy at the higher price.

Offers that your prospects can't refuse don't leave anything to their imagination. Every aspect must be spelled out completely. Confusion or complexity will kill your offer faster than readers can say NO! Compelling offers may take a whole paragraph or two or even more to spell it out in crystal clear detail. I often work them in immediately following the headline. In fact, many times my headline is merely a lead-in to the offer. Then, the remaining copy is just a process of elaborating on and giving factual and emotional support to the offer.

When you have a particularly strong offer, you can often increase response by mentioning that offer in your headline. You'll skyrocket your profits if you get really good at crafting offers your target market can't refuse. Practice writing dozens of "deals". Take ads you see in magazines, sales letters you get in the mail, or from email or web marketing you see and improve their offers. Create powerful offers with immense promise, complete believability, and then pile on the benefits!

Another Way to Make Your Offers Stronger

You can increase sales by reducing the fears that your customers may have just before they buy. A guarantee that is both clearly stated and easily understandable will go a long way towards easing those concerns. Just as with headlines, guarantees can be made more powerful if written in an interesting and compelling way. Here are two examples for an imaginary product, the Buzz-Cut Razor, to illustrate two different ways of stating a guarantee.

Example #1:

"The Buzz-Cut Razor is fully guaranteed for one year. If you are not satisfied for any reason, we will refund the purchase price."

Factual, logical, descriptive... and that's fine. But we can do better...

Example #2:

"Your Buzz-Cut Razor is fully guaranteed for life. Use it to save serious money instead of sending your husband and the boys down to the barber shop for expensive haircuts. You'll save enough cash every month to take your family out for a pizza, salads and drinks on a Saturday night and get a night off from the dishes! And if for any reason you are ever not completely satisfied with it, just give us a call toll-free and we'll take care of it for you right away. We'll arrange for a replacement and provide return shipping OR refund the entire purchase price if you wish. This is a no-hassle, unconditional lifetime, 100% money-back guarantee."

See the difference? Can you "see" the pizza? Can you smell it? Can you visualize your family in the restaurant? The second example also clearly explains how the guarantee works and what happens if you need to call, putting the prospect's fears to rest that they might be ignored when they have a problem.

Write your guarantees like this and they will definitely be more effective and compelling than plain old boring ones... leading to more sales for you!

Better guarantees almost always increase response rates. If you were selling 150 units of a $99 product for every mailing and getting 6% returns on a $30 (your cost) product, you would have a cost of returned good of $270. (9 returns x $30). If you strengthen the guarantee and increase returns by 50% but at the same time boost sales to 200 units, you'll increase revenues by $4950 and increase returns expense by a paltry $135. I'll do that deal all day long... wouldn't you?

A Final Thought about Offers

Highly successful marketers don't sell price. They sell value. Price will always seem high if value is perceived as low. When copywriters focus on price either because of poor product knowledge, poor client knowledge or poor sales skills, they will always generate less profit in the long run. Clients don't want cheap. They want the best value for their dollar. If you are focusing on price you will never sell all you could.

However, if you always sell value you will never have to worry about losing business to price competition. Sure, you might lose a sale here or there. But if you are in this business for the long haul for both your company and your client, sooner or later your prospects or clients will come back to you and the value they need and desire.

I once crafted a deal that offered seminar attendees a $49.95 manual for signing up by a certain date. The offer was big and believable because we had sold that manual for more than a year at that price. The price of the two day seminar was $299. We sold scores more registrations than normal. It was a clear success by any measure. But here's the kicker! Those manuals didn't cost us $49.95. Since we were the publisher and printer, they cost us less than $6 each. Six dollars for $299? Pretty good ROI, wouldn't you say? Think about what that could do in your business.

Now you have all the keys to creating your own irresistible offer and watching your profits soar. Just keep adding value and more bonuses until you come up with an offer than makes your prospect feel that they're crazy not to order!

6: Ask Them to Do Something Easy

Even if you feel in your heart of hearts that your sales copy is extremely well written, it will be a waste of time and money if it doesn't cause your prospects to immediately take action on your offer!

Part of this assumes that you have made an emotional connection with your reader. (Covered elsewhere in this book.) The rest of it boils down to the case you have made for the urgency.

How to Make Your Prospects Take Action Now

There's no doubt about it, a lot of us put stuff off. After all we are terribly busy now and will get to things later. Right? But, how many times have you thought you might like to buy something, decided to do it later, put it aside, and then totally forgot about it? Or worse yet, picked up the offer again days later only to realize that you really didn't want it after all?

That's why you must convince your prospects that they will experience some sort of loss if they don't buy right away. I like to accomplish this by using some kind of deadline or scarcity factor to make prospects take immediate action.

If prospects think an offer is going to be around forever, there's no reason to act quickly. That's the reason deadlines work so well. When I was writing direct mailers for seminar providers, I would clearly state as part of the offer a discount of $70 off the regular seminar price if people would simply sign up more than 7 days in advance. Just before that seven day deadline arrived we always had a spike in business. But that wasn't all... for the next 24-36 hours we would have people call begging to do business with us at the lower price. That's exactly what we wanted them to do!

Pick up today's newspaper or a current edition of your favorite magazine. Count the number of ads that don't ask for immediate action. Marketing messages without a clear, convicting call to action are a lot like a salesman who never tries to close the sale. In other words, you must ask for the order!

There are a number of ways you can close the gap between action and inaction. Not all work equally well... as these examples will show:

The first is what I call the "whenever" call to action. In terms of effectiveness, it's not much better than nothing. More importantly, if you are selling something that is expensive or purchased infrequently, it's almost always hopelessly ineffective. This type of call to action doesn't give the reader any compelling reason to do anything. It seems almost like an afterthought.

Consider an ad for an air conditioner that carries the "whenever" type of call to action like… "Stop by or call your local dealer". How likely is anyone to do that unless it's 100 degrees outside and their old unit just broke down? Not very likely at all…

The second type of call to action can be called "get them involved" copy. A common example of this is asking the prospect to fill out a form that assess their interest in (or need for) the product or service. It might go like this:

"Ask yourself this question. If you answer yes, call us today for a free estimate…"

This type of call to action is a little better than the first one. It may hold the prospect's interest a moment longer, but still doesn't MOTIVATE them to DO something that moves them closer to actually writing a check to you! There still remains the gap between convincing the reader that they need your product or service and them actually doing something about it.

The third and most viable call to action involves asking the recipient to do something that will either act by a certain time or at least identify themselves as a prospect. Here's a checklist for you:

- Asking for a free sample by a certain date

- Requesting a free booklet or report by a certain date

- Agreeing to a free trial by a certain date

- Free installation before a certain date (urgency)

- Limited supplies

- Limited time discounts (Give expiration date)

As you can see most of these have some sort of urgency kicker. In my own experience the shorter the time you give them to respond, the better the response. Seven days is about as long as I'll ever go. (In the case of email this is even more the case... most of the sales will come within 2 days, so limit them to that if you can. Here's a tip... I've have increased email response rates by sending another reminder email shortly before the expiration date.)

7: Sales Letter Mojo

Letter writing seems to have become a lost art. Before the telephone, people were much more skilled in written correspondence. The most important details of relationships, finance and government were conducted by letter. Letters were valued and saved. Many became resource material for history books. Not so today. When was the last time you received a personal letter in the mail?

However, sales letter writing is a money-making skill that can easily be learned. For purposes of this book, we'll divide sales letters into two main types...

First are personalized letters that have been written directly to and for a specific prospect. They are usually part of a two step campaign designed to get an appointment or induce the recipient to request additional information.

  and ...

Direct response letters/packages that usually are sent with presort first class or bulk rates to thousands of recipients all receiving the same message. These letters/packages are most often designed to result in an immediate sale.

We'll look at both types in detail...

Personalized Prospecting Letters

Personal prospecting letters are most often used to move the prospect closer to a buying decision. Here's an example of an ACTUAL sales letter that I actually received about a year ago. It may not be so different from many that you get in your own mailbox every week. I kept it in my files for just this chapter and just for you. I've changed their name to protect the guilty:

February 4, 2xxx

Dear Mr. McCraigh,

Pronounced Presentations is a large, international provider of audio/visual equipment and services; specializing in large corporate productions. We are very eager to work with your organization on any events you may have in the future.

"Pronounced Presentation's strength lies in our customer support, product knowledge, and state-of-

the-art equipment. Our staff has over 20 years of experience and our technicians are fully trained and authorized in setting up XYZ Projection, ABC Audio Systems, and 123 Support Interfacing.

Pronounced Presentations hopes to provide you with an alternative to hotel audio/visual companies. Pronounced Presentations firmly believes..."

Enough already! Every paragraph starts off with their company name. It's all about them. You get the picture. I threw it in the trash but then pulled it back out to share with you. Read on to see how to craft letters that will get the results you want.

Headlines and Sales Letters Openings

Since the beginning of this book dealt extensively with developing headlines, you may suspect that I will suggest that you use a headline on personalized prospect letters... If you do, you are absolutely right!

In school, we all taught how to properly format a letter. It starts off with the date, inside address and salutation. It's warm and gentile. You remember... something like this:

April 23, 2xxx

Ms. Paula Prospect, CEO

ABC Company

123 Main Street

Anytown, USA 10000

Dear Ms. Prospect,

A hot summer is just around the corner. As a business owner or manager, you realize how important it is to minimize summer cooling costs. This year is sure to be no different.

While I was writing this section, the Microsoft Word® Assistant appeared on my screen and asked me if I wanted it to help formatting a letter. Usually, it's extremely helpful, but in this case a traditional format is not what you need to cut through the clutter of hundreds of other marketing messages.

The example above does absolutely NOTHING to capture the attention of a busy prospect. Why? Because it states what the reader already knows... Summer is hot and it's coming again this year. So what? There's no reason to keep reading. In our "two second" society, you have got to get to the point faster than ever. If you begin your letter with boring, meaningless generalities and don't make your point in the first paragraph, you will lose the reader forever. And into the trash your letter goes... along with your postage and printing costs... Ouch!

Successful copywriters start their letters with a headline that packs a punch and openings that hit the ground running. Here is some copy I wrote for a utility company, aimed at CEOs and business owners whose buildings had older, inefficient cooling systems: (Notice how different it is from the "traditional" Paula Prospect example above.)

Cut Your Air Conditioning Costs by up to 48% this Summer without Spending a Dime Today

Save almost half on your cooling costs this June through August with our HVAC replacement program that's meant to save you cold, hard cash.

And there is no need to pay for anything now...just call before 5:00 p.m. May 6th to arrange a no cost evaluation of your current system. But call NOW, as we can only install 32 systems with this city sponsored program...

They "sold out" all 32 systems within 12 days. Such is the power of a good headline followed by a strong opening. I told the reader everything they needed to know by the end of the first paragraph. The rest of the letter simply supported the contentions in the opening material. And there was no "Dear CEO" line!

More on Openings

Someone once said that people most remember the material they read first and last. What comes in between is important, but it doesn't stick with readers the way beginnings and endings do. The first paragraph of a sales letter (or web site, or brochure, or ad) MUST accomplish two things:

• Grab the reader's attention.

• Get directly to the point, NOW.

When the beginning paragraph is direct and interesting, the recipient will likely read the entire letter with care. If the paragraph rambles on or is unclear, the reader will likely skip the rest of the letter... and you guessed it... throw it into the trash.

So, put your biggest bang in the first paragraph. Make sure it really says something by getting to your message fast. Too many writers mistakenly use this paragraph as an "ice-breaker" or "handshake" section to establish rapport instead of addressing the business at hand. (Like the "summer is here" example above.) The opening must KEEP the reader's attention earned in the headline. Rewrite your opening three, four or even more times, making each subsequent version better. Do that as many times as needed. Offer the Reader Something Right in the Opening... Like a free booklet, free trial or product sample. Make sure it is clear there is no risk or obligation on their part. Use this as a "door opener" not a "sales closer".

Organizing the Rest of Your Letter

The body of your letter should restate the message you are trying to communicate. Most business buyers will read a lot of copy as they are constantly on the lookout for information and advice that can help them do the job better, increase profits, or advance their career. Consumers will also have no problem reading long copy if they think it will improve their condition!

Your prospects are hungry for information and respond better to letters that explain what the product is and how it solves a particular problem for them. Don't be afraid to write long copy in mailers, ads, and brochures. Prospects will read your message... if it is interesting, important, and relevant to their needs.

Use Parallel Construction

What do I mean by parallel construction? There are two kinds of buyers, analytical types who will study your letter in detail before committing... and spontaneous types (like many creative marketers!) who often buy on impulse. The idea is to create parallel tracks through your letter so that the analytical types can scrutinize and the impulsive types can skim your letters (or ads, or brochures or web sites!)

How to you do that? By using subheads to summarize the main point of each detail section. Professional copy writers know that subheads highlight major points in the body of a sales letter. Use subheads to keep the spontaneous types interested longer and reading more and more of the letter. Think of it as "sound-bite" writing. Like this:

Subheads Can Pay Huge Dividends

Notice how this section topic has been centered? It stops your eye and makes the point even though you don't read the entire paragraph following. Any time you can spend learning the art of writing great subheads will almost always pay back dividends in terms of increased sales. Need a source of good subheads? Look no farther than those 15-20 headlines you wrote in search of the perfect lead off to your sales letter! Subheads should act to summarize the paragraph immediately following them. This helps readers skim your letter quickly and get right to the most important points.

Using Prospecting Letters to Generate Leads

A one-page letter is far too short to effectively sell products or services. In fact, your goal should not be to make the sale in a single step. Your goal is to generate a response, whether it is a return mail card, a fax, an e-mail, phone call, or fax. You just want a lead at this point... because you can't count on getting the sale from a single page prospecting letter.

This leads us to our second type of letter, those designed to get the sale the first time out...

Direct Response Letters

Direct mail letters are almost always designed to make the sale on the spot and need to contain far more information than a prospecting letter designed to simply move a prospect closer to a sale or appointment. As a general rule of thumb, the longer the direct sales letter, the more it will sell. I once received a 16 page sales letter, read the entire thing twice and bought what they were selling in complete confidence. No short letter could ever do that.

How long should your letter be? Long enough to convince the reader to act. People will read a 16-pager if it is benefit-oriented, interesting, easy to understand and well laid out. On the other hand, they won't get through a short one-page letter that's boring, slow to get to the point, or difficult to read. There's an old adage that says: "the more you tell, the more you sell." When it comes to direct mail, that's absolutely true.

If you are trying to make a sale, and the reader has never heard of you or your product, you may have to write AT LEAST four or more pages to get your message across. (Actually this would be one piece of 11 x 17 inch paper folded in half to 8.5 x 11 inches.) Don' be afraid of length. People will read any length of copy AS LONG AS IT IS INTERESTING to them! A good direct mail sales letter consists of the five elements we covered earlier in this book. These are:

- The headline

- The opening

- Proof of claim

- The offer

- The close

Tips for Improving Your Direct Mail Results

- Use a deadline to increase the rate of response so the recipients understand they have only a limited time to act.

- Make it easy for prospects to respond in a way they find comfortable for them based on their own personal style. Give them your phone number, fax, URL and email address. Include a postage paid business reply card or envelope. Don't sacrifice a sale for the price of postage!

- Use typewriter type (courier) for your printed letters to older prospects. Nothing makes your message look more warm and personal than a letter that appears to be typewritten, *especially* for older prospects. If your prospects are younger, use something more modern.

- Use short, easy words. Most of your words should be six letters or less. Keep paragraphs short. Four to six lines seem to work best for me as dense copy discourages readers. Use bullet points (like this list) to quickly showcase important items.

8: Building or Renting Lists

The next statement may seem a bit odd in a book about copywriting, but it is one of the most important things you'll read in its pages. Like my comments about headlines, skip this part and you'll miss an incredibly important piece of information worth many hundreds of times the price of this book.. Now that I have your attention:

The most important part of your mailing will be your list!

Not the copy, the paper, or the envelope. This is true for sales letters, catalogs, subscription offers, bicycle accessories, nutritional supplements, seminars, books, and services... whatever you can name. Get the email or snail mail list wrong and your response rate can easily drop under what's profitable... no matter how well-written and attractive your marketing piece is. It's a lot like the age old question, "If a tree falls in the forest and no one is nearby to hear it, did it make a noise?" Except in this case we are talking about members of your optimal target market (OTM) "hearing" your message.

60% of your snail mail and email success comes from your list, 30% from the offer and only 10% from all the rest. The best lists are almost always comprised of members of your OTM that know you, like you and trust you. They have purchased from you before, (or better yet more than once... It costs 6 times more to win a new customer than it does to make a sale to an existing customer.)

Next best are people, who by their behaviors are similar to your customers. For example, a list of known buyers of bicycle racing equipment would be a good potential list for a catalog of bicycle racing books and accessories. Compare data from your own customer base in terms of these attributes and develop a profile based upon actual purchasing patterns.

Here's a Checklist for Renting a Snail Mail List

Use an experienced list broker who is familiar with your industry. These brokers are generally paid by the list owners, so take advantage of their knowledge and experience. Select a list broker much like you would a Realtor, interviewing two or three and finding one you're comfortable with. It can be the start of a profitable relationship!

Always ask about the "recency" of a list. When a list has not been purged (or "cleaned") for 12 months or more, returns can rise to unacceptable levels. Most list owners will guarantee deliverability up to 95%, others only to 93%. Save all returns to insure that you know what your return rate actually is. CD-ROM directories offered for sale online and in some retail stores can be many YEARS old. Once, while looking through mail returns with a client, I found one addressed to myself at business address I had used 5 years earlier. The suite of offices I had once rented at that address did not even exist anymore... it had been remodeled into part of another suite!

Ask as to the "specificity" of sort. Common list "sorts" include SIC (Standard Industrial Classification) codes, employee size, ownership of certain software, political contributions, annual sales, magazine subscriptions, zip code, gender, and on and on. The closer you can come to your OTM, the better the response will be.

Always de-dupe (remove duplicate names or "records") a list both against itself and any other list you may be merging it with. Postage and printing is expensive. Why waste money and irk the recipient with two or more copies? Sophisticated de-duping programs, (designed to find and purge duplicate names) are now available from most mail houses. The best ones still allow you to send to multiple names within a larger firm, but eliminate all other unnecessary duplication.

Use an experienced mailing service to transfer your rented list to the mailing piece or envelope. Along with your list broker, they can be one of your best allies. Postal rules for larger mailings have become increasingly complex over the past few years. Mailings must be sorted and prepared in a very specific manner to qualify for presorted first class or bulk rates. Since postage will normally be the largest portion of your mailing expenses, paying too much for postage can quickly eat away at your profits. To get the best postal rates, most mailings today need to be bar coded before mailing… something that is difficult to do on your own. Also most mail houses have software that will certify mailings per current postal deliverability requirements... something else that's impossible on your own unless you make a large investment to bring that capability in-house. Unless you are a very large mailer that will never pay off. So use a mail service!

Here's another good reason to use a mail house. If a bulk mailing is submitted incorrectly, the Post Office will either return the mailing to you for correction, or offer to mail it at the normal first class rate. A rejected mailing can spell financial disaster. For an initial mailing to a cold list, this can be the difference between making and losing money on a project!

When I was actively mailing, (in some years we would send out well over 1,000,000 pieces) I would always stop by the mail house after our mailers arrived there from the printer. That would give me a chance to inspect them one last time as well as make sure they were matched with the correct mailing list. Those visits would also give me a chance to get to know the staff on a first name basis and insure the mailing was right.

If you maintain your own in-house list use a database program to manage that list. It also allows you to export your data into a comma or tab delimited file formats to your mail house for merging, sorting, and de-duping. (Some rental lists come with prohibitions against merging with another list. Check with your broker on this.)

Test Mailings

I once had a colleague that didn't feel that he had the time to test mailings before they were sent out. Everything was always a big rush, last minute, and deadline driven. The risk of error was enormous. Thousands of dollars were on the line. Changes were made capriciously and without regard for hard test data. I was glad I wasn't in his department. He never seemed to get the improvement in response rates he longed for. There was always a "reason why"... the weather, the competition, the season, the printer, the paper, the ink color... tides... sunspots. You get the picture.

In the final analysis it was his undisciplined approach. He was driving blind. He may have well taped thick, brown paper pages on his car windshield and driven in the highway like that... An accident waiting to happen! Untested direct mail can be a huge money-loser if done haphazardly. The list of things that can and do go wrong are endless. Experienced mailers know this and always test potential mailings to reduce risk.

Testing Your Snail Mail Lists

As discussed elsewhere in this book, your list will account for the lion's share of the success of a mailing. In order to get intelligence on what your response rate might be without committing to an entire mailing of say 200,000 pieces, it is best to test a list.

Testing a list involves sending the actual piece to 5000 names on the list to determine what kind of response you get. If it is well beyond your breakeven, then you will be happy to produce and mail the balance of the list. If not, you will have saved yourself and your company significant money. Almost all list owners and brokers will allow a test quantity. If not, you should ask yourself why.

If you are testing a list, ask for an "Nth" select as opposed to the first 5000 names on that list. If the list is sorted by postal code, all of your test pieces will go to the same area, an area which may or may not well represent your target market. For example, all the mailers might go to a large city, when your offer may turn out to most appeal to rural markets. An "Nth" select will pull records from throughout a list rather than one section. For example, if a list you are considering renting has 250,000 names, to yield 5000, you would select every 50th name. (Here the value of N=50. 250,000 divided by 5000 is 50.)

After the results are in from the 5000 mailers, you can research the orders to determine if you really did do better in rural areas as opposed to cities.

Segmenting Your List for Better Results

The most successful direct response marketers vary their pitches based on the type of prospect who receives it. This time-tested technique is based on setting a specific objective based on each type of reader.

One way to classify these marketing objectives is to break them down into three areas: Awareness, Trial and Usage. (Often abbreviated ATU in marketing-speak). Let's discuss Trial and Usage first and skip Awareness for now.

Trial devices are sent to non-customers with the objective of converting them into buyers. These often take the form of coupons, discounts or premiums for new customers sent to rented or cold lists. These types of initial trial offers typically have lower response rates because in most cases the prospect has never heard of you or done business with you before. This makes for a harder sell... sometimes requiring a deeper discount... but as long as you are converting non-triers to users at a profitable or at least breakeven rate, trial offers can be great house list builders. Since you are writing a specific trial offer, you can deal directly with issues that are known barriers to trial for what you are selling.

Usage devices (sometimes referred to as frequency builders) are sent to already existing customers into purchasing more often than has been their normal pattern. Examples here are "buy 10 get one free punch cards" or discounts for buying multiple units at one time. The good thing about frequency offers is that they can produce higher response rates because your audience doesn't need to be convinced to do business with you the first time. They are already happy with you and more likely to do business with you than a cold name on a rented list. (It's almost always been easier to build frequency than get trial by non-customers... And you don't have to give up as much to get the reader to respond!) These types of pieces can be written more specifically to convince the recipient to repeat a known favorable experience. You can even further subdivide this group into light or heavy users with separate offers to each. In my experience, the more specific you can get when copywriting, the better your return on investment (ROI) will be.

Back to Awareness... it has no place in direct marketing. For the most part Awareness messages serve only to transmit information. For example, a bank might send a reminder that they have just opened a new branch in your neighborhood or a stockbroker might send out a letter saying that they now offer IRAs. Good customer service, but it really won't do much for revenues. Response will always be better if you have a specific and targeted offer.

Designing Your Mailing Piece

You may have a piece or package you have used for a while that seems to be working out OK, or you may be building one entirely from scratch. It might be as simple as a postcard or as complex as a multi-step campaign.

Your first step will be to create a realistic looking mock up of the piece. Color desktop laser printers now make this easier than ever. Years ago, graphic designers had to create these by hand... a long and tedious process. Today, there is no excuse for not coming up with 3-4 variations.

If your mailing does not consist of a standard postcard or number 10 envelope CHECK WITH YOUR POSTAL SERVICE before handing the job off to your printer. You may fall outside of postal regulations. If that is true, they could require additional postage that destroys your profit in the job, or worse they could reject the mailing entirely!

Besides size, shape, the final weight of your piece, weight is a very important consideration. Go over the maximum allowed and you'll pay additional postage, reducing or even eliminating your profits on the mailing. If you are anywhere close to the maximum weight over which extra postage would be due, be sure to construct your mock-up of the SAME paper and envelope stock as you will use for the actual job. Often, the paper used by your commercial printer will be heavier than what office supply stores sell as laser printer paper. I once supervised a job were the printer substituted another paper sock on a close tolerance job and we had to wait for the moisture to evaporate out of the ink during a rainy week in order to mail it!

All postal sectional centers in the US have at least one person who is a helpful expert in these matters. Get to know them. They can often offer a wealth of excellent suggestions. Get their approval to suspect pieces in writing before spending precious resources on printing. This is one time not to go to the internet, go to the Post Office Sectional Center in person with a sample mock-up!

Make your letter as easy to read as possible. The best letters have one thing in common... they look good and are easy to read. If your letter is not easy to read chances are that the prospect will simply trash it.

Timing of Your Mailing

When to mail is always a big question. Here are some tips that will help you make that decision. Mail your letter so it gets delivered on a lightest mail days. Often, these days are Tuesday and Wednesday. These are the lightest mail days in the U.S. and having your letter delivered on the day they receive the least mail increases your likelihood of the piece being opened and read. Avoid Mondays. Monday is often the heaviest mail delivery day in this country. Why take the chance your response rate will be lower?

Response Rates

Don't assume a single mailing will generate the response you want. A good mail program contacts the prospect multiple times each year. Consider mailing at least quarterly if you want the prospect to recognize and respond to your mailings. Single mailings, while they can be profitable, will almost always be less profitable than a series of slightly different messages that are not merely a duplicate of the previous letter.

Doubling Date

Here is a helpful "rule of thumb" for measuring a mailing's response. A mailing's doubling date is at that point in time when 50% of the returns for the mailing can be expected to have been received. So if your normal doubling date is 7 days, then on the 7th day after the first response is received you will have received half of all business you will get from that mailing. The rest will trickle in over a period of months and even up to a year unless there is a hard deadline built into your offer. This assumes all pieces are mailed on the same day and reach the prospect about the same time. This can be a little more difficult to determine if you are using bulk mail, but helpful if you need a quick read on a mailing.

What is a Good Response Rate Anyway?

The conventional wisdom in the direct mail business says: Half of all sales letters get thrown away before they reach the prospect, another 50% of the remaining half get thrown away by the prospect without so much as a glance. Still another 50% of the remainder will get discarded after having been opened and examined but not read. Of what is left only half get read and then immediately thrown away. Another half yet are put aside to be thrown away later. In some cases, if you get a 1% response rate you are doing pretty well.

But here is the important thing... It doesn't really matter. You can have a 10% response rate and still lose money on a mailing. How? Because it is not about the response or "capture" rate, but the gross margin on a large mailing. A good mailing should return at least 3 times the expenses associate with it. It's about PROFIT... not response rate!

The Mailing Package

First things first...In my experience, self-mailers almost always FAIL. These are generally in the form of tri-fold pieces that are comprised of a single piece of paper sent without an envelope. Why? Because there is generally not enough information included to cause the recipient to make a purchase decision! A typical direct mail sales package will include five critical components: the letter itself, the envelope, an order form, a lift letter, and a reply mechanism(s).

A lift letter is a small note, usually folded to about 3 x4 inches or so that is printed on colored stock. A lift letter usually offers "one more reason to buy" or carries a headline that reads "If you have decided not to buy". Think of them as sort of a postscript on a separate piece of paper.

The closing of your letters should typically seek to encourage the reader to take some specific action such as making a decision, forwarding a reply, or correcting a problem. In many ways the closing of a letter parallels the opening. Both should be short, to the point, and specific and should be free of overused, passive phrases that do not communicate much. This call to action is critical to your letter. It's also important to let your reader know when to take action. A simple "Please call me by next Tuesday with your answer" may be all that's needed to secure the response you want.

Whenever possible your letters should specifically state what action is expected of the reader and by when. This dated action increases the changes that your reader will respond as requested.

When I was in the banking business I quickly learned that "The older a past due loan payment gets the colder it gets". It's the same for marketers... the longer a prospect goes without buying from you; the less likely he is to buy anything at all.

How many times have you thought you might like to buy something, decided to do it later, put it aside on your desk and days later totally forgot about it? Or worse yet, decided you wanted it after all and couldn't find the ad to save your life?

That's why you almost always need some kind of deadline or scarcity factor to make your prospects take action now. If your prospects believe an offer is going to be around forever, there's no reason to take action. That's the reason deadlines work so well.

Deadlines usually work better if they are specific and relatively short term. If you have done a good enough job of copywriting, the reader will earnestly believe they can't live without your product. A firm and quick deadline will help you produce more sales based on their fear of losing out on a good deal. As I've said before in this newsletter series, people will often do more to avoid loss than they will for a prospective gain of the same amount. Make that fact work for you!

Limited availability kickers work best when they are absolutely believable. I use them only when they're really true. (Which isn't very often.) But, there is a way to do this if you are in a business with unlimited supply... Offer a fixed number of units for a special price. When they're gone, they're gone. This is an especially useful technique when you need to raise some fast cash. If a customer asks for the deal after the allotted number of units run out, simply make an "exception" like we did in the seminar business.

Pick up today's newspaper or a current edition of your favorite magazine. Count the number of ads that don't ask for immediate action. You'll be shocked. A marketing message without a clear, convicting call to action is like a salesman who never tries to close the sale. He'll go through the motions with little if anything to ever show for it.

When you finish what you want to say, stop. Many people feel compelled at the end of a letter to add routine phrases like, "If you have any questions please call," or "I hope this answers your question," or "Please give this matter your careful consideration." Avoid these all-to-familiar platitudes which sound neither sincere nor friendly and are overused and tired. Unless you have other important topics to discuss, just end your letter with a simple call to action and your signature. If there is nothing more to say, simply end the letter... do not feel it is necessary to ramble on about unrelated or personal topics. Good sales letters are written as though the writer of the letter is having a personal conversation with the reader, not like formal business correspondence.

Using a Post Script

The second most read part of a sales letter is usually the Post Script or P.S. It will often be much to your advantage to have one (or more) Post Scripts at the very end of your letters. Use them to restate your offer along with your key benefit and guarantee, assuring the prospect that they are making the right decision to act. Here are a couple of examples:

P.S. You will save $50 if you are among the first 100 orders. Your order must be received by our office no later than Monday June 3rd.

P.S. While it still fresh in your mind, return the order form today and we'll rush you the exclusive book "How to Save Big Money on Printing" as our free gift to you.

P.S. This seminar is not for everyone. Please understand that there are only 30 spaces available. Once these spots are filled, that's it!

The P.S. is prime selling space. Be sure to take advantage of it!

The Look and Feel of Your Letter

Visual attractiveness accounts for 75% of your letter's impact. Put this on a PLAIN piece of high quality paper. That's right, PLAIN but make it the best you can afford. Cheap paper sends a subtle, but clear message to the recipient. Don't clutter it with your logo and other extraneous stuff at the top… that's for your headline. Put your contact information below your signature.

Use enough white space, resisting the temptation to cover every square inch of the page, giving your reader a place to occasionally rest their eyes. It is hard for the reader to wade through lots of endless text. Use short paragraphs. Use bulleted or numbered lists to make points. Give the reader a break. Make it easy for them to get through the whole letter. Make your letter look as personal as possible and sign it yourself with blue ink. Keep it to one page. Most company presidents, buyers, and homemakers are busy. Make your point, sell the benefits and make it easy to read. Your readers don't have lot of time.

Final Words on Sales Letters

Have your sales letter proofread...then have it proofread again. Make sure everything is correct. Just one tiny, seemingly insignificant typo can destroy the credibility you worked so hard to build. Typos can be more than embarrassing; they can scuttle an entire campaign. One pizza delivery restaurant I know once sent an expensive mailer to households in the surrounding zip codes. Results were horrible. The reason why became very evident when the woman whose telephone number had been erroneously printed on the mailer called to vehemently complain about all the misdirected calls she was getting!

Kiss of Death Sales Letters... do this and surely fail!

Start by introducing yourself and your company. Begin by writing about how great your product is, how long you have been in business, and how good your prices are. Skip anything remotely related to the reader, their problems, and how your product will benefit them.

Finally... usually, one letter doesn't get it done...

Often, it's not a single piece of mail that wins the business. Rather, it takes a series of letters, brochures, ads, and mailers... to turn a cold list into paying customers.

Fighting Writer's Block

Stuck? Start by putting together a detailed features and benefits sheet and write your offer first. Once you have that, your sales materials will practically write themselves. Then look at some of the fill-in-the-blanks examples in this book.

Getting it Opened

If your envelope is never opened, your direct mail offer will fail. Consider using a printed teaser on the outside of the envelope. Often I'll repeat the headline or a variation of it on the envelope.

Use metered mail or computer printed postage. You will find some controversy on this subject, but individual stamps and metered mail are opened at the same rate and get virtually the same response according to recent studies. This will ensure your recipient knows he or she is receiving a business letter. In business to business mail, metered mail is not only acceptable, it is considered professional. Today, many business envelopes with individual stamps signal a letter from someone looking for a job.

Definitely avoid using pre-printed permits (indicia). Studies show that 30% of bulk mail sent to large corporations is NOT delivered internally. Instead mail presorted first class with a postage meter imprint. (This is another reason to use a good mailing house.) While it is cheaper to use third class postage, you'll often cut your response rate enough to negate any savings.

9: Crafting Profitable Print Ads

Why does one ad succeed while another one fails to generate little if any results? It can be due to a single missing element, an overall lack of a clear offer, or simply running it in the wrong place at the wrong time!

A Time Tested 4 Step Formula

Just as a building needs a solid foundation to stand over time, a good ad needs to be well constructed to be effective. Throw something together quickly and both the house and the ad are bound to collapse under their own weight. The AIDA formula has been around for a long time for good reason… it works. In the introduction to this book, I said that many of the old rules don't apply anymore. This is not one of them. It is critically important that you follow these four basic rules of marketing and advertising. Ignore these for critical elements at your own peril:

- Attention

- Interest

- Desire

- Action

Now let's look at this time honored formula in terms of the five elements we covered in Part One of this book and bring this 4 step process into the 21st century:

Attention

This is not rocket science. You must get the prospects' attention if you want to sell anything. Attention must be the foundation of your ad or any other sales piece. How do you accomplish this? Use a headline to reach out and demand that attention! (We dealt with this extensively earlier in this book. If you skipped it go back and read it now!) If an ad has a headline that is weak or nonexistent, readers will pass it by without a second thought. In today's overly busy, self-centered world, unless your ad talks to the prospect... and fast, it will be a waste of your time and money.

Interest

Once you have the prospect's attention, you can begin to build interest. In the process of creating your ad or letter, you will next want to gain the interest of your target buyer, the person you wish to sell to.

Your task is to draw them in FURTHER with an opening that holds a compelling grip on them. Interest is normally gained by tapping into the emotions of your prospect. Another important way to fuel interest is through stories or testimonials of happy customers. Interest is what keeps prospects reading and staying involved with your message. Keep their interest by showing them the benefits the product or service in a way that will make things easier or solve a problem for them.

"Our great tasting granola bars will give you an easy way to lose weight."

"This eye cream will help you look younger and more rested."

"This policy will save you money over what you pay now"

Desire

The third step is to build an insatiable desire for your product or service in the mind of the prospect. The main tool you'll normally use to do this is the "offer". Marketers build desire by creating a tremendous "just-got-to-have-it-now" feeling for their product or service. You know that you have constructed a truly compelling offer when people feel like they are "losing out" if they don't buy now. I try to make my offers so irresistible that prospects just have to say yes:

"These roofing materials are half price until the end of this week, and after that you'll have to pay full price. No exceptions."

"Buy this insurance policy before May 3rd and we'll make the first 2 months of premium payments for you... absolutely free!"

"Why toss and turn another night? All of our mattresses can be delivered to your home today with no interest or payments until June of next year"

Action

Many ads forget to close the sale. You have to ask people to buy! If you've given them a reason to buy, a slew of great benefits, strong guarantees, and great bonuses, ask for the sale!

Make it easy for them to buy. As a rule of thumb, the easier it is to buy, the more orders you'll get. Tell them exactly what to do in order to place their order... *"Call toll free within the next 10 minutes"* or *"Fill out the simple form below."*

Using Logos

Logos have but one function in an ad, sales letter or brochure... to act as a "signature" to identify the company. NEVER lead with your logo on the top of the page. I know of one company who puts their logo on the front of all of their brochures. Who cares? NOBODY! It violates the rule of A.I.D.A.

If you have built "brand equity" in your logo, it can serve another function, that of adding credibility to your offer. The State Farm Insurance logo certainly carries more weight than "Joe's Insurance Agency!" Even if this is the case, that brand equity type logo should go in a lower position. The reader, not the writer is central!

Pictures and Illustrations

A few years ago I was helping a group of chiropractors who wanted to improve the response that he was getting from his mailings and brochures. I read through what they had been using and found the copy points pretty well written. But, what caught my eye was the illustration they had been using… it was a very negative image that detracted from their offer. It depicted a man bent over in pain, with what appeared to be bolts of lightning shooting out of his back. They explained to me that the picture was used to illustrate the problems that their prospective patients were experiencing.

I suggested that they instead illustrate what their patients were SEEKING, not what they wanted to eliminate. I said that the prospect KNEW they had pain, what they were looking for was a timely SOLUTION! Once they agreed, some additional probing uncovered the fact that many of their patients were younger women, many in their 30's. I asked them what those women wanted as a result of their treatment. With some research, we determined that what they missed most as a result of their back problems was the ability to pick up their children! We had a photographer provide us with some shots of mothers holding their children and incorporated them into the brochures and posters. Response rates increased by nearly 210%.

Photos should only be used to clearly illustrate the benefit of what you are selling. Make it a picture of what people want and you'll connect with them on an emotional level. The best pictures are almost always of the product or service in actual use by people enjoying its benefits.

Avoid clip art at all costs. There is no clip art that hasn't been used a thousand times or more. It will do nothing but cheapen your brand image. Few things will make you look more amateurish than overused clip art!

If you want to buy some high quality stock photos for your projects consider online vendors like http://www.fotosearch.com or http://www.istockphoto.com where you can search different vendors of quality stock photographs. Note the varied individual pricing policies of the suppliers, as price can sometimes vary depending on how you use the photo. Some vendors offer non-royalty photos, usually a good bet if you are on a budget. If you are going for something more unique, royalty art will be the way for you to go... it is less likely that readers will have seen it someplace before. (I have no business relationship with either of these firms, other than as a customer.)

Placing just one or two carefully selected images within your materials can be worth thousands of dollars in sales. Any images in your sales copy should complement the copy itself and add to your overall sales message..

A well chosen image will almost always more than pay for itself!

Using Humor in Ads

Avoid humor. It rarely ever works. (Yes, we covered this before, but it bears repeating!) Why? Humor is often dependent on a common experience for people to "get it", of which your prospects may have very little. In some cases it may actually offend people. With so much riding on your offers these days, why risk it. It does nothing to convince your prospects to part with their hard-earned money.

More Tricks to Increase Response

Here are some ideas you can test to improve the response rates of your ads. These ideas fall into my "rule-of-thumb" category… meaning that they work in most cases:

- If you're using one photo or illustration, make it a relatively large single image to draw the reader's eye. If you must use more than one photo or illustration, it's usually best to make one significantly larger than the rest. Designers will tell you to use an odd number of elements for a look that's more pleasing to the eye. I agree.

- Always use captions under photos or illustrations because they have extremely high readership rates. Use this space to tout the benefits.

- A BIG, up-front in-your-face offer will almost always outperform an offer hidden in the fine print.

- Response by offering a variety of reply mechanisms… Toll free numbers, web sites, physical address, mail and fax. Make it easy for people.

- Color almost always boosts response unless you have a horrible piece.

- Use lots of benefit subheads. Readers of ads usually spend precious few seconds scanning an ad to see if it's of interest.

10: Creating Money Making Brochures

This is one of those places in this book where I am going to tell you something worth far more than the price you paid for it. Perhaps hundreds or thousands of times more... Here it is:

You will without a doubt turn your brochures into much more potent sales tools by applying direct marketing techniques to them. This means adding attention grabbing headlines, informative subheads, strong proof of claims, and "knock their socks off" offers to get more flat out response than you ever would from a standard "image" piece. In other words, write and design your brochures like sales letters!

When you really think about it, almost everything you do should be direct marketing based. People who think that such an approach ruins their inspired copy or artistic layout must erroneously value image more than results. They are misguided... And they will always sell far less than you will!

Brochure Basics

Well-written, money making, results getting ads, letters, brochures and web pages all have a lot in common. While there are differences in the details, the methodology used to construct all of them is pretty much the same.

If I were sitting down to help you with brochure design, here are three questions I would ask at the outset:

What's on the front panel?

The cover of your brochure will be the only part the prospect ever sees if you don't grab their immediate interest. The number one error most brochure writers make is to design a front panel featuring primarily the firm's name and logo. Do you have any brochures like that on your desk now? Probably not… because you've probably thrown them away already!

When I assist clients with brochure design, I almost always use a strong headline on the front panel along with a photo illustrating the main benefit I'm communicating. Selling ice chests? Forget about your logo... Use a picture of a smiling user reaching into one and pulling out an ice cold drink on a hot summer day. If you must put your logo on the front cover, stick it in a lower corner, like a signature. Most logos belong on the back along with your contact information.

Inside, the most persuasive brochures usually have photographs of real people actively using your product to amplify your body copy. Consider using before and after shots (or "with" and "without" pictures) to fully dramatize the benefits of using your product. Selling degreaser? Why not show a pleased mechanic using your product contrasted to one struggling without it?

How do you intend to use the brochures?

Is it a leave behind piece for outside sales reps? Will you be mailing it in response to requests for information about your products? Will retailers be using it as point-of sale material? The reason why this is so important is that your brochure should meet prospects where they are in the sales cycle. For example, outside reps contacting existing customers need a brochure that effectively recaps what they have said during a face-to-face sales call. It might focus more on the new products than on your company, since they are already familiar with your firm. On the other hand, if the brochure is mailed to prospects that are not even remotely aware of your company's track record, more space might be used to help overcome objections to doing business with an unknown vendor. It is also helpful to know if the brochure will be a stand-alone piece or accompanied by other elements such as a sales letter. This will have a bearing on how much information you include in the brochure itself.

Does it connect the product's features to its benefits?

Most brochures do a good job of listing product or service features, but don't tie those features to the benefits of owning or using it. One way to think of your brochure is as a sales letter with pictures. A good sales letter has an objective... to motivate the reader to purchase your product or service. Compelling benefits are what move readers to the next step... be it a purchase, an appointment, or a simple request for more information. Most brochure copy I review these days seems to incorrectly stress features over benefits. We covered this in the chapter on headlines, but it bears repeating here:

Features ... "What products and services have"

For example, "This accounting software has a payroll module"

Advantages ... "What those features do"

For example, "This accounting software will allow you to do your payroll in your own office"

Benefits ... "What the advantages mean"

For example, "You will save time and money over using a payroll service"

Benefits appeal to a desire to gain something, such as increased income, social status, security, love and to help avoid undesirable things like pain, financial loss, unnecessary work, or embarrassment. Contrary to popular thinking, clearly communicated benefits are not vehicles for creating hype or puffery. They are an effective means through which customers can fully understand and appreciate your offering's true value.

Without demonstrating compelling benefits, readers won't care!

11: Power Editing Your Sales Copy

We have covered a lot of ground since page one. We still have a way to go, but it is worth pausing here for a moment to think about editing sales copy once it has been written.

I usually get two or three notes a year from writers, editors or school teachers who zealously point out that some of the stuff I've written falls short of their standards for "good English". I say... SO WHAT?

Don't get me wrong, I appreciate good grammar as much as the next person... but not at the expense of sales. My goal here is not grammatical perfection, but to produce the maximum amount of profit possible. But, you can't buy groceries with perfect punctuation!

I can't argue with the fact that faultless form is essential when we write to prospective employers, college admissions officers or others we need to impress. But in sales letters, direct marketing pieces, or in ads "proper English" can actually weaken your materials... and can be downright dangerous for your bottom line! Let me explain...

Well-written sales materials are conversational in tone and sound more like how we talk than how we write. If we edit away informal warmth and friendliness, sales copy can start to sound stiff or forced, alienating the reader. When you stop to think about it, most of us do speak in partial sentences, one-liners and even single words. That's what can make a foreign language so hard to master, because real people don't speak or write like schoolbooks. They speak in little "sound bites" to clearly communicate in the most efficient way possible... just like good copywriting should.

A lot of times, when asked to approve sales copy, many people will take out their red pen and start marking it up for grammatical errors while missing the whole point... Will this copy sell product or not?

Last week I saw a sign in a restaurant window that read "Warm Apple Pie with a Double Scoop of French Vanilla Ice Cream." It made my mouth water... I could just taste the tart, warm fruit mixed with the cold, sweet ice cream just by reading the sign. I was sold by an incomplete sentence!

Editing Copy for Better Response

So consider editing your copy to make it easier to read, more appealing to the senses and more believable... not for textbook perfect form. It's OK, even desirable, to use sentence fragments, one sentence paragraphs, and sentences that begin with taboo words like "or", "and", or "but" to grab and keep the prospect's attention! Feel free to use capital letters, indents, bullets, quotation marks, ellipses (...) and exclamation points for emphasis. Short thoughts and tight phases will make your point faster and keep the prospect reading longer. Let the excitement you have for your offering show through in your copy. You may take some grief from bosses and self-appointed critics, but they'll soon come around when they see increasing sales and profits! Here are some more tips to keep in mind when editing and polishing your work... Does it:

Promise a big, bold benefit in the headline and then deliver?

Draw the reader in right away and make them keep reading?

Read easy with large text, underlines and highlights?

Use small words instead of big ones?

Have extra words edited out to read faster?

Use short sentences and short paragraphs?

Use subheads that allow readers to scan?

Create a desire on the part of the prospect to take action?

Use bullet points to summarize key points?

Have a strong offer that the prospect can't refuse?

Contain specific proof of any claims it makes?

12: Writing Effective Web Copy

By the time you have read this far, you might be tempted to assume that writing for the Web is exactly the same as writing for print. Nothing could be further from the truth! There are two HUGE differences...

- People read differently on the web than they do on paper

- People are not the only ones doing the reading

Studies have shown that people read about 25% slower on computer screens than they do when reading a conventionally printed paper page. In fact, most people don't actually read online content— they scan it. In order keep your visitor's attention, your web pages must be extremely easy to read.

TIP: The basics of my five step method still apply (see the beginning of this book). Keep them in your copy. However, there are other things to think about in writing for the Web.

At the same time, your pages must also be written to be "search engine friendly". This means as often as possible work in key words and phrases that fit current search engine criteria. Having pages that rank well with the 3 major search engines... Yahoo, Google and Bing is extremely important. I'll deal more with keywords and phrases later in this chapter.

A Winning Web Strategy

Website visitors are hungry for information, particularly if they are looking for something they want or for a way to solve a problem. So, if you can get them to read beyond your opening headline, they are probably a pretty good prospect for what you're selling. This again points to the obvious... that you will have more success with your web site if you use direct marketing techniques than other methods. The key is that you provide enough detailed information to readers that they feel comfortable making a decision to buy your product or service.

The good news is that it is a snap to provide this type of detail on the web. It doesn't cost much at all to add additional pages that your information hungry visitors can devour. When someone visits your site, they are looking for information that is of high perceived value to them. If they find a link that interests them, they will click through to it. As they reach successive pages, they will repeat this same process as long as you continue to pass their test. This is just like sales letters where your objective is to keep their interest and keep them reading. The longer they read, the more likely it is that they will buy something. I'll elaborate more on this as you will see in the next few pages.

Before we go too far in terms of the actual writing of web copy, let's take a quick look at four different types of commercial website organization… and which one might make the most sense for you. These are:

- Content sites (without direct response copy)

- Catalog sites

- Sites that consist of only direct response copy

- 2 Step Sites with follow up mechanisms

Let's look at each one:

Content Sites without Direct Response Copy

This is the most popular type of web site, but tends to be the least effective if your objective is to sell lots of your product or service. These types of sites tend to have pages and pages of content designed to appeal to search engines. They are leftovers from the dot-com days when "eyeballs" were all important, and marketers believed that if enough people looked at their site, they would make money.

Don't get me wrong, content is still important from two perspectives...

First, it is true that having content will make it more likely that you'll get better search engine rankings which will lead to more traffic. But if you are do not provide a strong call to action on your site; you won't be maximizing the return on your investment of time and resources.

Secondly, good content helps warm up the prospect because it helps position you as an expert. People are more likely to do business with someone they trust as knowledgeable. But there is one other critical thing that these sites typically lack that limits their profit potential... a follow-up mechanism. A site without any kind of follow-up relies on a single opportunity to sell and will always be less successful than it could be. More on this later...

The only real exception to this rule are websites that have a huge amount of off-line promotion such as those of television stations, professional sports teams, consumer products companies with a national brand presence or well known national organizations.

Catalog Sites

Catalog sites, as I call them, consist of straightforward listings of related products for sale. There is usually little in terms of content on these sites. Each item is normally pictured with some description and is linked to a shopping cart. To be most successful, sites like this usually need to have a lot of off line promotion to make them work. Unless the item is hugely unique in terms of its basic nature or price, you are competing with thousands of others... not a happy proposition! (An example of a highly unique site that could succeed as a catalog site might be one devoted to downloads of alternative or underground music... something very definitely different by its very nature.)

Catalog sites can work well for established retailers who also have an actual physical location and a well established off-line customer base.

Sites that Consist of Direct Response Copy Only

Now we are getting "warmer" for those who sell one thing (or perhaps a very few related items). There is an old adage in sales that says that you can only sell one thing at a time. Some of the most successful sites on the web are DRC (Direct Response Copy) that feature only one compelling offer and are literally comprised of only one long page of sales copy. These sites have no content per se, but are really 10-12 page sales letters online. These are not actually "pages", but one single web page that the visitor scrolls down as they read... the equivalent of those 10-12 printed pages.

For the investment of your time and money, a single page with direct response copy (or landing pages on an existing site) will almost always outperform a multi-page content site. There is still a place for content laden sites for serious marketers, but only as "click magnets" to drive traffic to your single page site or landing page.

2 Step Sites with Follow up Mechanisms

Here is where the deepest profit pools lie. Two step sites offer a combination of not one but two single sell pages. The first page is designed with only one thing in mind… getting the email address of the reader. The page has no other function. Normally, such a page will offer something of value… a multipart course, a free e-Book, or other valuable information of interest to the visitor. The copy is written in such a way as to convince the visitor to trade their email address (or even more contact data) for that information. There is no attempt to sell whatever product the marketer is selling, just get the email address or other contact information. The premise of this method is based on something that direct response marketers have known for years… that a list of people who have expressed an interest in a specific topic will always outperform a list of cold names.

Back to the methodology... Once you have obtained that email address, the visitor is served up the second step... another single sell page in which you do offer your main product or service. There is a good chance, given the right copy, that you'll close the sale right then. But here is the secret... now that you have their email address, you can continue to send communications in the hopes that they will eventually buy from you. And many of them will. Far more in fact, than if you had taken just one shot at them during their first visit to your site.

I tend to favor multi-part "courses" in the subject matter related to your product your service. (Although I will do small eBooks at times) This will give you multiple opportunities to warm prospects to your offer, even vary your offer for those who do not buy immediately. This is a powerful way to sell when coupled with an automatic follow-up mechanism.

Most really successful online business could not make the money they do without automated follow-up. Imagine trying to send immediate and personal emails to all of the people that respond to your offer of a free course. You can't do it. But you can automate the process with autoresponders.

Autoresponders are simply computer programs that will automatically send a specific email to a specific email address. If you are a programmer, you could try to do this yourself, but most of us are not. The good news is that a number of really good online providers that are often inexpensive and will more than pay for themselves. Try MailChimp.com or AWeber.com. (MailChimp will let you have up to 2000 list members for free.)

With an autoresponder, you simply "pre-load" it with messages and set the date on which it is to be sent to your prospect. Here is an example of how this might work:

In exchange for their email address, you offer visitors a free 4 week course in how to fly-fish. Once they sign up for the course, you set your autoresponder to send them 4 separate emails, one every Thursday until they have received all installments. The autoresponder then takes over the job of sending out the emails automatically... even while you sleep!

Each of your course installments would provide the information that you promised, along with information about your product or service and a link back to a single sell page where they can buy it.

So instead of just one chance to sell them something, you have 4 including the second sell page! And here is the beauty of integrating your autoresponder with your purchase records... if they buy the product on the second sell page, you can change the message that they receive with their four week course to another product... or no sales message at all if you have only one thing for sale.

I have to tell you that you will want to have a second product! People who buy one thing from you are highly likely to buy another. After a time, you can "wear-out" or saturate a list... especially a small one with just one product.

Constructing Results Getting Web Pages

Before we spend a lot of time writing and organizing, it's helpful to visualize what your finished pages will look like.

The Look and Feel of Your Web Pages

Reading on a computer screen is very different than reading on paper. Your web pages themselves should be white or light in color to provide good contrast between the text and the background. Reversed text (light words on a very dark background) will make your site hard to read. Light colored text on a light colored background is even worse! If you want bright, bold or oddball colors on your site, save them for the graphic elements, not the text.

Have your web designer use tables to keep your page widths about 600 pixels wide. This enables your pages to display pretty much the same regardless of your visitor's settings.

For good font choices, go with Arial, Verdana, Tahoma and Times New Roman. These are all easy to read on the web. Save the wild and crazy typefaces for logos and other graphic elements. Left justified text with a ragged right edge is best. Avoid underlining web copy unless it is a link. And skip the italics… they're too hard to read.

Write for How People and Search Engines Search

More and more these days, especially with Google, the key is not so much your meta tags, it's the copy that's clearly visible on your site's pages. Write to be found for what people are searching for. That means using the keywords and phrases that your target market is using.

Before you begin writing, you need to sit down and plan the keywords you will use in your content. There are excellent websites that will help you do this... Wordtracker.com and Google's Adwords Keyword Tool

Both have tools to enable you to see which keywords are most popular and therefore most useful to you. You have to dig a little in these sites but it is worth it.

Big, Bold Money-Back Web Guarantees

A guarantee for what you're selling in any medium is essential, but for the Web it is extremely important. People need to know they can get their money back if something goes wrong. This is extremely important when they're buying something on the Web. They don't know you. You may live in a different country, with different consumer laws. They can't see their purchase until after they've paid for it. So people naturally want a strong guarantee (and the stronger the better!) before they hand over credit card information. Without a strong guarantee you will surely lose sales.

TIP: Want to have some fun getting ideas for your own site? Check out the Webby Awards. Adapt some of the creative ideas to what you are doing!

13: Social Media Hacks

Social media advertising is a complex process that requires effective planning, testing, and measuring. Done right, FaceBook and Twitter ads can be incredibly effective for your business. So why is this section near the back of the book? Because everything you have learned so far will be tested when writing ads for social media. When writing social media or even pay per click copy (Google Adwords) it is critically important that your message is made crystal clear in the limited amount of characters allowed. For example with FaceBook, your ad must include a headline and is limited to 25 characters for the headline and 90 characters for the body text. Twitter is of course limited to 140 characters. In my experience the number one reason why social media venue ads fail to produce the anticipated results is because they are too VAGUE.

As I wrote earlier in this book, our number one focus should be on headlines. This is doubly true for social media were the headline can be most if not all of the ad. If readers don't get past the headline, they never get to the order page.

In traditional copywriting, effective headlines must get right to the point in ways readers can't resist acting on. But, in social media we have so much less space than in a paper ad or sales letter. We must strip out extra words to meet character count requirement. That makes it harder. How do we do that? By dropping adjectives and adverbs that sound great but rob precious space. The good news is that avoiding adverbs and adjectives helps build authority because we are not puffing ourselves up. What to use instead? ...Strong active verbs that show positive action and change.

In "The 100 Greatest Advertisements" by Julian L. Watkins shows that 95% of the most effective headlines from the early years of magazine advertising were eight words or less. This is because magazine copywriters had to write tight headlines due to space concerns. Well-written short headlines can have incredible money-making power, so go back and review the section on headlines in this book... you will have an unfair advantage over those who try to simply brainstorm good headline ideas!

My WWW Acid Test for Social Media Ads

When writing this type of short copy for social media, make sure your message answers these three basic questions:

Who is this ad specifically targeted to? (Age, gender, and interests)

What is the main BENEFIT (Review the section found earlier in this book.)

Why respond to the call to action? (Like protecting your health, being accepted or saving money)

Photos are Critically Important

Pictures are important in traditional ads... but even more important in social media. So with tiny character counts allowed on social media sites, your picture will be required to do a lot of the heavy lifting. You can write the most dazzling headline and body copy in the world, but if your pitch doesn't catch a reader's eye, you won't get any clicks. Use the best quality images you can find. If you can, avoid generic stock photography that we've all seen a thousand times before. Whatever you do, don't use your logo. You may love your logo, but no one else cares... trust me! Focus on the unique and interesting photo that says "read me"!

Images of people usually work well. Try to use close-ups of attractive faces that resemble your target audience. And try to use pictures of people in the same age range as your prospects. Images of people should face right into your ad text.

Getting the Words Right...

With so little space due to character count restrictions, it is more important than ever that we get the words right. From Takipi's (http://blog.bufferapp.com/data-backed-copywriting) research, we can adopt some ideas from something similar... the world of blogging. According to their research, the most popular blog posts had these words in their titles:

smart

surprising

science

history

hacks (or a variation like hackers)

huge/big

critical

If you're looking for reshares and retweets (and who isn't?), you might want to include these twenty most-retweetable words/phrases:

twitter

please

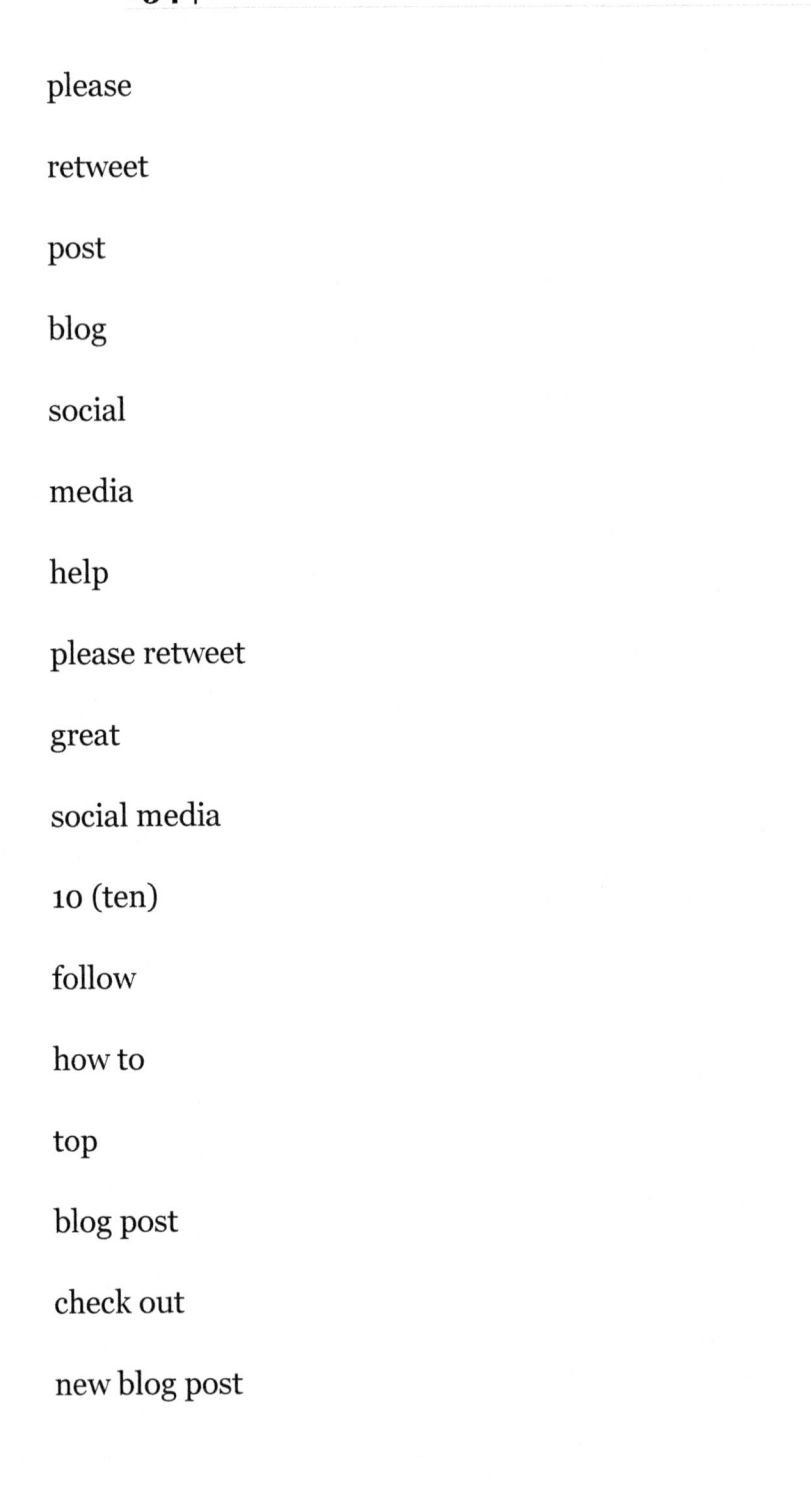

retweet

post

blog

social

media

help

please retweet

great

social media

10 (ten)

follow

how to

top

blog post

check out

new blog post

Takipi's study also found that using the word *you*, which many of us (myself included) assume is one of the most powerful words we can use in copywriting, actually didn't have any effect at all on how many social shares a post received.

More on Twitter

With Twitter, you'll be miles ahead if you craft tweets like you're having a conversation with an old friend. For me, I try to "write like I talk". That makes me unique and sometimes a bit unexpected. It's that different perspective or point of view that will set you apart and get attention.

Why this is so important? There are three types of Twitter ads...promoted accounts, promoted trends, and promoted tweets. The one you'll probably use most will be promoted tweets. These are messages that appear in the timelines of the specific types of users you target and at the time of day you bid on. But here is where really good copywriting pays extra dividends... Twitter rewards advertisers who create persuasive tweets by lowering their cost per engagement based on the click through rate of the Tweet. The more people click on a promoted tweet, the cheaper it becomes! If a tweet is receiving a lot of retweets, favorites, or replies it just gets better from there. Conversely, low performing tweets will cost more and make you less or even lose money.

I like to build my tweets for ease of retweeting. I do this by counting characters like this: My Twitter handle is @JimMcCraigh. That's 12 characters long including the @ sign. Then I add 3 more for the RT and the space which follows it and I get 12+3=15.

So the absolute longest tweet I would ever want to send is 140-15=124 characters. You can figure your own count. Your username will be different, so compute that number. The basic idea is to leave room for the extra characters that come with retweets. This protocol is of course subject to change from time-to-time by Twitter themselves, but just as you got used to 140 characters, you will get used to maybe 121 or whatever you end up with.

Now that we agree on that, I'm going to ask you to *drop another ten characters* down to about 111. This is really important because according to recent Hubspot data, (http://www.elevarmedia.com/blog/new-retweet-data-tweet-character-length) the number of retweets drops off sharply at about 111 characters. Click on the Hubspot link to see a graph of what I mean.

You Must Rotate Your Ads Regularly

One of the biggest issues advertisers deal with on many social media sites is ad fatigue. This means, when people start to see your ad too many times, they get bored with it and stop clicking through. For some reason, this is especially true on FaceBook. Like Twitter, when your click through rate starts to drop FaceBook penalizes you, driving up your cost per click and making likes, comments, and click-throughs more expensive. This means you will need to have more than one ad if you are going to advertise on these sites for more than a few days.

TIP: Your followers don't want to be annoyed with endless sales pitches, they want to be entertained, interact and have fun. Less than 5% your social media posts should be promotional in nature. Do more and you'll start seeing the unfollows start to pile up. Abuse and you'll lose!

14: Wildly Successful Email

The good news is that email is an incredibly cost effective way to reach your prospects. The bad news is that email is an incredibly cost effective way to reach your prospects. These days, there is a never ending invasion of spam that not only irritates us all, but some of it contains nasty viruses. Since its inception, there has been no other medium that has become so abused so fast. Despite all of this, your prospects are still interested in receiving what they consider to be useful information. But, there are ways to get through to them...

In spite of the problems, email is here to stay as a viable way of reaching those prospects who have given us permission to contact them. In fact, marketers who track open rates report that they have not experienced significant change on those open rates over the last year. Some have actually reported slight increases.

What does seem to make the difference is content. In other words, is the message relevant and persuasive? If it is relevant it will work, if not... it won't.

Getting your Email Messages Opened and Read

Let's start by emphasizing a point that I cannot make strongly enough. All of the techniques covered in this book relate to PERMISSION BASED email that is sent to a list of people who have specifically requested to receive email from you. Besides making bad business sense, spam (unsolicited commercial email) can and most often will get you banned from your service provider. Enough said.

Email Subject Lines... A Specialized Headline

What do headlines have to do with email? Subject lines are the first thing email recipients see along with the sender's email address. To make sure your email messages are more likely to be read by your targeted recipients, turn your subject line into a mini-headline. However, the purpose of an email subject line is somewhat different than your regular headlines... it is to get your message delivered to your prospect, and then to have them open it.

Forget trying to fool someone into opening your email message. Subject lines that try to deceive recipients will only annoy them. If you want them to open your message, craft a genuine communication that helps them solve a problem or meet a pressing need.

Writing email subject lines is much like writing any other type of headline, EXCEPT you must make sure your message makes it through spam filters.

Use Your Own Name

According to a recent study released by DoubleClick.com, your "From" line is listed as the most important factor in nearly 60% of survey respondents decision to open emails or not. All of the emails I send come from me, under my name and from a single email address. Over the years my subscribers have become very familiar with my communications. Being consistent with your "from" line and email address will help significantly increase the likelihood that your email reaches your prospects. In fact, in every message that you send, I highly recommend that you ask the recipient to put your from email address in their address book, trusted sender list or "white" list, depending what email service or program they use. As a trusted sender or contact, your email will easily make it through spam filters.

Using Email to Market to Top Level Executives

It sounds good, doesn't it? After all, it's free and easier than calling. Just send out 50 or 100 emails a day and the sales will start rolling in right? Maybe not. In fact, it's easier to

LOSE senior level executive prospects with email than it is on the phone!

Avoid using email for prospecting among top level executives and decision-makers. They are not typically heavy email users. Most of the people using email are staffers and managers, or owners of smaller companies. So, unless your email is from a source that they willingly agreed to get, you're going to be immediately deleted as spam if not by their software, by their assistant. If they perceive you to be a spammer, they will avoid further communication (of any kind) from you.

To successfully email these top level executives and decision-makers, you must have to build an opt-in (permission) list. How do you get that permission? The old fashioned way is still the best... direct postal mail (postcards can be used as well) to a high quality list directing them to a page on your web site. Keep the URL as short and simple as possible. These days, top level executives and decision-makers are more than willing to go online to reply via a form than ever before... IF they perceive that you are offering valuable information.

Don't make prospects fill out contact information each time they respond to one of your offers. Don't force them to enter a user name or password to enter your landing page. (Yes, I have seen that!) It's ridiculous to ask top level executives and decision-makers (or anyone for that matter) to jump through hoops to respond to your marketing campaign.

Resist asking for their email address without clearly noting what it will be used for. In this case it is best to advise them you will use it only for contact on an irregular basis only for information that they would find valuable. Always advise that their email address will not EVER be shared with anyone else for any purpose. Once you've gotten a top level executive and decision-maker to join your list, forget about sending a promotional newsletter or other sales information. Instead, here are some better suggestions:

- An invitation to a breakfast roundtable with some of their peers or a well-known speaker.

- A short web-cast or webinar they would find extremely helpful

- A one or two page PDF file containing information that is of high perceived value to them, but not in any way sales oriented. Have links in the PDF back to your web site.

Once top level executives and decision-makers allow you the privilege of emailing them, always respect their time, keeping your message short and focused on using the emails only to continue to develop and expand your relationship.

Thank You

I'd like to say thank you for purchasing this book! I know you could have picked one of many others on Amazon, but you took a chance with mine. So thank you for purchasing this book and reading all the way to the end. If you liked what you read, then I need your help. Please take a moment to leave a review on this book on Amazon. This feedback will allow me to write a kind of books that will help you grow your business!

BONUS SECTION

Here are three bonus sections that will pay you back many times the cost of this book. Consider it my thank you to you for purchasing it.

Stories Sell

One of the most powerful techniques you can use to illustrate the benefits of your product or service is to use a dramatic story where your product is the hero and saves the day for a customer. If you have been in business for any time at all you should have plenty of stories like this. (Haven't been collecting them? Now is a great time to start!) Here is one of the most famous examples of that potent copywriting technique. It has been used with great success for years by the Wall Street Journal (yes, that staid financial publication Wall Street Journal). It is the story of two young college graduates, one of whom subscribes to the Journal, the other who does not.

As the story unfolds, one of the graduates goes on to have a highly successful career in business, rising to the top and enjoying all the benefits that go with that level of success. The other seems always to languish at the bottom rung of the corporate ladder, moving from one low end position to another… never quite seeming to make it. The difference of course is the first graduates investment in a subscription to the newspaper that continues his business education well beyond college. It is simple story, yet a highly effective one. They've used it for years.

Here is another example of that technique when used to create demand for rental office furniture:

Not long ago, two start-up companies rented office space in the very same building. Today, only one of them has a thriving business. Customers seek them out by word-of-month advertising. They are adding new employees every month to handle increasing volume. And the company is hugely profitable with their sights set on future expansion.

The other company is a different story. Little money is available for marketing since profits have been elusive. Sales have been in further decline since the firm had to lay off salaried sales staff. The future of the entire enterprise is in serious jeopardy.

What was the difference between these two companies that once held such high hopes? The second loaded up on very expensive office furnishings, lots of staff, and luxury company cars so they would "look successful" to prospective customers. They were essentially betting that they would turn a profit before burning though their first round of funding. Not so smart! The first firm jealously guarded their seed capital and was prudent in managing expenses. Instead of buying expensive office furniture, they rented it from us here at ABC Used Office Furniture. They paid employees mileage for use of their personal cars. They ran lean on staff until new hires were absolutely necessary. Very smart!

You get the idea. I'm sure that if you have been in business for any length of time you have a story or two to tell. Can't think of one? No problem, just ask your customers!

The One Word that Can Move Mountains

Over the years, there have been a number of experiments done to prove this word really does what it purports to do. And I have never seen one that disproves it. Most of the studies involved asking a stranger to do something for a study volunteer, like lending them money. The variable was how they were asked. Usually two nearly identical scripts were usually prepared, one using the word and another not. The scripts using that word almost always outperformed the one that did not. Curious to know what it is? (It is not the word please or the word free.) So OK, here it is…

Script 1:

College student to a passing stranger in the library...

"I wonder if you might lend me 25 cents?"

Almost every person asked this way declined. Now here's the script with the word added:

Script 2:

Same student to a passing stranger in the library...

"I wonder if you might lend me 25 cents **because** I need to make a copy of a page for a class that starts in 10 minutes? That's **because** my grade depends on it!

With the word because added, almost every person asked this way was happy to help. (The student using script 2 actually had two "becauses", one that explained why they needed the quarter and another that stated the consequences.) It seemed that most people he asked didn't want to be responsible for his going to class without what he needed!

Think about how you can work the word BECAUSE into your sales copy. It is a true response booster. The profit implications could be huge. Since direct response marketers work on typically slim margins anyway, a small increase in response can often lead to a big increase in profits!

Logic Tells and Emotion Sells

There is always an emotional component to every sale, even for hard-nosed corporate purchasing agents. In other words, if the prospect does not become EMOTIONALLY INVOLVED in your message, the odds of converting them into a paying customer are against you. This is true for anything you sell from autos to zippers. Even highly paid CEOs buy on emotion and then use logic to justify it later. If you want to craft effective sales messages you'll need to supply an emotional element as well as a logical one.

Most of us have no problem with the logic part. After all, we know our own product or service inside out and backwards. But how do you draw the prospect in emotionally? Prospects don't care about you, your company, or what you're selling. What they do want to know is: "What will I gain or lose if I don't act NOW?" Convince them by proving that you can help them in at least one of these three areas:

- Meeting a Pressing Need

- Solving a Severe Problem

- Satisfying an Intense Desire

Which of these three areas does your sales copy address? Think about it. These are the basic reasons people buy. Even impulse buyers fit into one of these three scenarios. Zero in on the one that is appropriate for your offer, create a compelling case around it and you'll markedly improve the results of your promotional efforts.

Skip this emotional component and your copy will be "flat"... and you'll definitely not enjoy the best possible results for your efforts. But if you can reach the prospect on an emotional level... step back and watch your revenues soar. You'll have more money to spend on advertising, but you may not need it!

Bonus Book Excerpt

From *How to Find More Customers and Clients with Webinars, Seminars and Workshops*

at http://amzn.to/1uLzM1S

Presentation Tips Designed to Boost Your Business

If you want to maximize the amount of business that you get from presentations, there are *three critical things* that you must say from the podium. Of course, we all know that shameless self-promotion never goes over well with audiences, especially if it is a paid presentation. But that is not what I am suggesting. Rather, I am going to propose more of a stealth mission for you...

You must tell them you are in business and that you have clients...

Have you ever heard a speaker give a great presentation, but fail to let you know that they are in business to serve clients?

I'm not talking about an overt commercial here... which is always in poor taste. Nor am I talking about handing out brochures or flyers which will ultimately end up in the trash. What I am saying is that weaving stories into your presentation that mention your business and clients will educate your audience as to what you do. I'm shocked at the number of speakers that don't mention it. Doing this is the mark of a true professional. You might say something subtle like this:

"To illustrate this principle, let me tell you about a client engagement I had about six months ago."

Or during a question and answer period...

"I had a client call me at my Berkeley office a couple of weeks ago and ask the same question, this is what I told her."

(Of course we will NEVER say a client's name and problem in the same sentence unless we have express written permission... doing so demonstrates that we will break confidences.)

Further reinforce this by using examples and references to past engagements you've done. One of the most powerful techniques you can use to illustrate the benefits of your product or service is to use a compelling story where you are the hero and save the day for a client. If you have been in business for any time at all you should have plenty of stories like this. (Haven't been collecting them? Now is a great time to start!) If you are a new professional, use examples from past jobs.

Here is one of the most famous examples of that persuasive technique. It's been used with great success in years past by the Wall Street Journal (yes, that staid financial publication, The Wall Street Journal). It is the story of two college graduates, one of whom subscribes to the Journal, the other who does not.

As the story unfolds, one of the graduates goes on to have a highly successful career in business, rising to the top and enjoying all the benefits that go with that level of success. The other seems always to languish at the bottom rung of the corporate ladder, moving from one low end position to another… never quite seeming to make it. The difference of course is the first graduate's investment in a subscription to the newspaper that continues his business education well beyond college. It is a simple story, yet a highly effective one. Stories make your presentation come alive and help your audience to come to know you better. Piles of brochures and business cards can't do that. Find your own stories and share them.

You must tell your audience how you benefit your clients...

Go a step further and let your listeners know how clients have benefited from working with you in the past. Benefits take the form of either achieving more of something or less of something else. Think higher profits, increased sales, more elderly served, better response times, finding the right career or lower utility bills, fewer accidents, less waste, fewer defects and lower taxes. You might say something like this:

"Let me give you an example here to illustrate my larger point... last fall I helped a company reduce their reject rate by 12%. You can too, if you follow these 5 steps I am going to cover next."

or...

"When I work with clients at their office or at times remotely by phone and a screen sharing application like Web-Ex or GoToMeeting... it's great because I don't have to get on a plane and the client saves money."

Talking about benefits in this way makes it clear to your audience that you make an impact, get results and help improve the client's condition. All good stuff!

You must tell your audience they will get a freebie of real value after the presentation...

I'm not talking about pens or candy here... but something that will directly benefit them. This does two things, first it keeps the audience engaged (they don't want to miss how to get it!). Secondly, it gives them something of greater value than a brochure... something they will likely keep. These freebies can range from physical booklets to books to real hardcover books if you have written one... to anything else you can think of. How you get it to them can vary, from free downloads to a pallet of your books in the back of the room. It is amazing how well this works. The object is that they remember you. Use the freebie to further demonstrate what you offer clients.

Talk about the freebie throughout your presentation to whet their appetites. Perhaps you can even get the meeting planner to pay for it.

Do these three things I just mentioned constitute some sort of audience manipulation? Hardly! It is a simple presentation of facts designed to help the audience understand exactly what you do and how you work while you give them the very best information available about the topic of your talk. Anything less is not in their best interest or yours!

What About Speaking for Free?

When this subject comes up in polite company, some of my fellow speakers go nuts! There is no way, they say that they would ever "cheapen" themselves" be doing free speeches. I not only think, but know they are dead wrong!

When I first started presenting seminars and workshops about 25 years ago, I did some paid gigs, but essentially would speak anywhere they would have me with no fee. Not only did that help me hone my craft as a speaker, but it helped me get the testimonials and referrals that I needed to progress to larger paid groups. I also met some great clients along the way. So as I see it I've never really done a "free speech", just some I didn't charge for!

Today, I need to be more selective with my time, but will consider larger groups comprised of my target audience if I feel the exposure would be worth my time. I do ask for basic travel expenses if it is out of town.

TIP: Sometimes it pays to join an association that is comprised of your potential clients. Not just to have the opportunity to present there, but as a way to serve that organization... in return, you'll learn a lot about your target market!

Like this excerpt? You might want to check out:

HOW TO FIND MORE CUSTOMERS & CLIENTS WITH WEBINARS SEMINARS & WORKSHOPS

JIM McCRAIGH
A No-Nonsense Marketing Guide

http://amzn.to/1uLzM1S

CPSIA information can be obtained
at www.ICGtesting.com
Printed in the USA
LVOW04s1823191115
463349LV00032B/1313/P